D1414364

NUNSUCH

Stories about Sisters

Collected by
Candida Lund

THE THOMAS MORE PRESS
Chicago, Illinois

PS648
.N85
N86
1982

Fiction
Nunsuchs
N86

ISBN 0-88347-139-6

ACKNOWLEDGEMENTS

Paul Horgan, "The Surgeon and the Nun"
   Reprinted by permission of Farrar, Straus and Giroux, Inc. "The
   Surgeon and the Nun" from THE PEACH STONE: *Stories from
   Four Decades* by Paul Horgan. Copyright © by Paul Horgan 1930,
   1935, 1936, 1937, 1940, 1942, 1944, 1947, 1949, 1950, 1951, 1952,
   1959, 1963, 1967; copyrights renewed by Paul Horgan 1958, 1962,
   1963, 1965.

Joan Vatsek, "The Bees"
   Reprinted by permission of the author. From STORY magazine,
   March-April 1942, and THE BEST AMERICAN SHORT STORIES
   1942, edited by Martha Foley, published by Houghton Mifflin Company. © 1941 by Joan Vatsek.

Katharine West, "Meditation"
   Reprinted by permission of the author and THE CRITIC, copyright
   by the Thomas More Association.

J. F. Powers, "The Lord's Day"
   Reprinted by permission of the author. From PRINCE OF DARK-
   NESS, published by Vintage Books/Random House. © 1943, 1944,
   1946, 1947 by J. F. Powers.

Frank O'Connor, "The Corkerys"
   Copyright © 1966 by Harriet O'Donovan, as Executrix of the Estate
   of Michael O'Donovan. Reprinted from COLLECTED STORIES,
   by Frank O'Connor, by permission of Alfred A. Knopf, Inc. First
   published in *The New Yorker*.

TABLE OF CONTENTS

Candida Lund	*Preface,* 9
Paul Horgan	*The Surgeon and the Nun,* 13
Joan Vatsek	*The Bees,* 36
Katharine West	*Meditation,* 51
J. F. Powers	*The Lord's Day,* 55
Frank O'Connor	*The Corkerys,* 65
Rose Tillemans	*Minutes of the Meeting,* 85
Joyce Carol Oates	*In the Region of Ice,* 90
Charles Healy	*Round Trip,* 113
Madeline De Frees*	*The Model Chapel,* 133
Brendan Gill	*Mother Coakley's Reform,* 151
Gerturd von Le Fort	*The Song at the Scaffold,* 159

* Written as Sister Mary Gilbert

Preface

A few years ago Ann Landers asked me to reply to a letter from a troubled young woman who thought she wanted to be a nun. I suggested to "Popular in Montana" ("I'm what you would call a popular girl with the guys. . . . Now I'm thinking of becoming a nun") that there were both valid and invalid reasons for becoming a nun. Valid reasons include (1) to serve God in a particular way; (2) to have fuller opportunity for prayer; (3) to live in a community with persons who share your ideals. Among invalid reasons are (1) to escape from a broken home—or to escape from anything; (2) to find an instant solution to your problems; (3) to believe that a change in life-style will produce a new you.

The concept of sisterhood, hardly as old as Eve, does nevertheless go back to ancient civilizations. Witness the Naditu women (chaste and living in community), who flourished in Babylonia in 1895 B.C. To this group belonged the sister of Hammurabi. And witness also, centuries later, but still before Christ, the Vestal Virgins in Rome. It was left, however, to the Roman Catholic Church to provide a framework, scaled large, whereby Sisters became a part of the general scene.

In part sisterhood rests upon the shared motives that impel some women to become Sisters. It embraces, however, more than that. Today the modal word best expressing sisterhood is "community," a beautiful word if not battered and bruised by over-use and over-stress. "Community" appears frequently in the stories that follow.

It is well-illustrated in Joan Vatsek's "The Bees," a tale of five Sisters in wartime. Driven out by bombings which

9

had killed the majority of their Sisters and leveled their convent, forlornly they return to their farm for an afternoon to care for the bees before leaving the village, perhaps forever. To go back called for courage. It meant seeing again their ruined home and being reminded even more poignantly of the Sisters who had met sudden death. It meant, too, that the beehives would be readied for winter, the drones picked out and trampled upon. As the Sisters began their work they could hear far-off bombing. Before they finished it stopped. "They all agreed that they had not even noticed it for the last two hours. They had enjoyed the communion of working together. They felt restored, whole once more. The little sisterhood breathed again as a unit."

Sisterhood sometimes shows itself in restraint rather than as a positive expression, for instance in "The Model Chapel" by Madeline DeFrees, then known as Sister Mary Gilbert. Views about the new chapel were varied and vigorous, "But Sister Constance, whose reservations about the chapel were equally strong, yielded her judgement and offered the sacrifice of seeming concurrence." It is also evidenced in the assured acceptance that Sisters take care of their own. The salty, even testy, old nun in "Meditation" by Katharine West was comfortable with this expectation and appreciative.

In other stories there are examples of "reaching out." As Paul Horgan writes of the nun in his classic tale "The Surgeon and the Nun," "She owned responsibility for everything that came into her life." In Charles Healy's "Round Trip" an old nun, very different from Horgan's Sister of Mercy, characteristically shows herself responsible for the stranger. Seeing a drunk or dying man lying on the pavement, she immediately crouched down and leaned close to him whispering comforting words in what were his last earthly moments. Her fastidious young companion, assuming the man drunk, pulled back in distaste.

Reaching out does not necessarily assure success. Joyce Carol Oates' story, "In the Region of Ice," tells of a Sister, a university professor, sharing the uncertainty and inability of parents to help their highly strung, suicidal son. One finishes the story thinking indignantly, "She should have been able to do something. She could have done more."

Contained in this volume are ten short stories and a short novel (or novella). The short stories generally portray women who are sturdy, energetic, faithful, dedicated. (It may not be an accident that all but one of the authors are Americans.) There is little of the spiritual odyssey in these stories.

Such is not the case with the short novel, *The Song at the Scaffold* by Gertrud von Le Fort (upon which is based the opera "Dialogue of the Carmelites" with music by Poulence and a libretto by Bernanos, based on his play.).

The novel has a haunting, lyrical quality making appropriate its music-related title. In the story the key figure—a young French aristocrat in revolutionary France—undergoes severe psychological suffering. Both as a child and later as a novice she is swallowed by fears. In the end she triumphs, and her triumph is one of grace.

A word about the term "nun." It is commonly used to mean any professed religious woman. Proper canonical usage of the word is limited in the Latin Church to a religious woman who has professed solemn vows or simple vows, temporary or perpetual, in a monastery in which solemn vows are actually or should be taken, and in which at least the minor papal cloister is observed. I have chosen to ignore the legal meaning and to use the word instead in generally accepted fashion.

Down through the ages Sisters have had a checkered press. Boccaccio (regarded by at least some Italian scholars to have been a devout Catholic—he almost destroyed the *Decameron* because of the unfavorable light in which it placed the Church) wrote of lively and lascivious nuns more interested in promiscuity with the gardener and available clerics than with the good of souls. Chaucer gave us a Prioresse who "leet no morsel from hir lippes falle" and who "was so charitable and so pitous, She wolde wepe, if that she sawe a mous Caught in a trappe, if it were deed or bledde."

And yet on the other hand a careful critic observed in *The New York Times* (1976):

> The strength of the Catholic Church of America is due more to nuns than any other single group. . . .their common sense, their hard work, their vision. . . . To them must be credited the success of the parochial school system, which is undoubtly the most important factor in the quality—and quantity, too, for that matter—of American Catholicism. Catholic higher education for women resulted from their efforts, as did a still vital chain of hospitals, and institutions of specialized care for the young, the aged, the homeless. Progressive movements in the Church, particularly social action, would never have outgrown the theory stage without them.

To carry out these works, nuns of intelligence, courage, faith, generosity have been needed. Some such will be found in this anthology.

Candida Lund
Rosary College
River Forest, Illinois
May 2, 1981

THE SURGEON AND THE NUN
by Paul Horgan

Here you are. I haven't thought of this for thirty years. I don't know what called it to mind. I'll tell you anyway.

When I was a young doctor just out of internship, I left Chicago to come West, oh, for several reasons. I'd worked hard and they were afraid my lungs might be a little weakened, and then besides, I've always been independent and wanted to get out on my own, and I'd seen enough of the society doctors back there. Anyway, I came on, and heard of a new section of country in New Mexico, opening up, down toward Texas, and thinks I, I'll just go and see about it. The hottest day I ever spent, yes, and the next night, and the next day too, as you'll see.

The railroad spur had been pushing down south through the Pecos Valley, a few miles a week; and it was in July that I got on the train and bought a ticket for Eddy, the town I was thinking about trying.

The track was completed all the way, by then; but they had a lot of repairing to do all the time, and no train schedule was maintained, because we'd move, and crawl, and then stop, baking, with nothing but dust to breathe, white dust like filtered sunlight; outside the car window was naked land—with freckles. I remember thinking: spotty bushes and gravel. Above, a blue sky like hot metal. The heat swam on the ground.

You couldn't sleep or read or think.

There was nobody to talk to in the car.

Two seats across the aisle from me was a Sister of Mercy, sitting there in her black robes, skirts and sleeves, and heavy starch, and I wondered at the time, How on

13

earth can she stand it? The car was an oven. She sat there
looking out the window, calm and strengthened by her phi-
losophy. It seemed to me she had expressive hands; I recalled the sisters in the hospital in Chicago, and how they
had learned to say so much and do so much with their
skilled hands. When my traveling nun picked up a newspaper and fanned herself slowly, it was more as if she did it
in grace than to get cool.

She was in her early thirties, I thought, plump, placid
and full of a wise delicacy and, yes, independence, with
something of the unearthly knowingness in her steady gaze
that I used to see in the Art Institute—those portraits of
ladies of the fifteenth century, who look at you sideways,
with their eyebrows up.

She wore glasses, very bright, with gold bars to them.

Well, the train stopped again.

I thought I couldn't stand it. When we moved, there was
at least a stir of air, hot and dusty; but at that, we felt as if
we were getting some place, even though slowly. We
stopped, and the cars creaked in the heat, and I felt thick in
the head. I put my face out the window and saw that we
had been delayed by a work gang up ahead. They were laborers from Mexico. Aside from them, and their brown
crawlings up and down the little roadbed embankment,
there was nothing, no movement, no life, no comfort, for
miles. A few railroad sheds painted dusty red stood by the
trackside.

I sat for ten minutes; nothing happened. I couldn't even
hear the sounds of work, ringing pickaxes or what not; I
felt indignant. This was no way to maintain a public conveyance!

It was around one o'clock in the afternoon.

Mind you, this was 1905; it isn't a wilderness any more

out here. Oh, it was then. Every time I looked out at the white horizon my heart sank, I can tell you. Why had I ever left Chicago?

Then I wondered where the Sister was traveling to.

It was strange how comforting she was, all of a sudden. I had a flicker of literary amusement out of the Chaucerian flavor of her presence—a nun, traveling, alone, bringing her world with her no matter where she might be or in what circumstance; sober, secure, indifferent to anything but the green branches of her soul; benign about the blistering heat and the maddening delay; and withal, an object of some archaic beauty, in her medieval habit, her sidelong eyes, her plump and frondy little hands. I almost spoke to her several times, in that long wait of the train; but she was so classic in her repose that I finally decided not to. I got up instead and went down to the platform of the car, which was floury with dust all over its iron floor and coupling chains, and jumped down to the ground.

How immense the sky was, and the sandy plains that shuddered with the heat for miles and miles! And how small and oddly desirable the train looked!

It was all silent until I began to hear the noises that framed that midsummer midday silence—bugs droning, the engine breathing up ahead, a whining hum in the telegraph wires strung along by the track, and then from the laborers a kind of subdued chorus.

I went to see what they were all huddled about each other for.

There wasn't a tree for fifty miles in any direction.

In the heat-reflecting shade of one of the grape-red sheds the men were standing around and looking at one of their number who was lying on the ground with his back up on the lowest boards.

The men were mostly little, brown as horses, sweating and smelling like leather, and in charge of them was a big Texan I saw squatting down by the recumbent Mexican.

"Come on, come on," he was saying, when I came up.

"What's the matter?" I asked.

The foreman looked up at me. He had his straw hat off, and his forehead and brows were shad-belly white where the sunburn hadn't reached. The rest of his face was apple-colored, and shiny. He had little eyes, squinted, and the skin around them was white too. His lips were chapped and burnt powdery white.

"Says he's sick."

The Mexicans nodded and murmured.

"Well, I'm a doctor, maybe I can tell."

The foreman snorted.

"They all do it. Nothin' matter with him. He's just play-actin'. Come on, Pancho, you get, by God, t' hell up, now!"

He shoved his huge dusty shoe against the little Mexican's side. The Mexican drooled a weak cry. The other laborers made operatic noises in chorus. They were clearly afraid of the foreman.

"Now hold on," I said to him. "Let me look him over, anyway."

I got down on the prickly ground.

It took a minute or less to find out. The little cramped-up Mexican had an acute attack of appendicitis, and he was hot and sick and, when I touched his side, he wept like a dog and clattered on his tongue without words.

"This man is just about ready to pop off," I told the foreman. "He's got acute appendicitis. He'll die unless he can be operated on."

The heat, the shimmering land, something to do—all changed me into feeling cool and serious, quite suddenly.

"I can perform an emergency operation, somehow, though it may be too late. Anyway, it can't do more'n kill him; and he'll die if I don't operate, that's sure!"

"Oh, no. Oh-ho, no, you don't," said the foreman, standing up and drawling. He was obviously a hind, full of some secret foremanship, some plainsman's charm against the evil eye, or whatever he regarded civilization as. "I ain't got no authority for anythin' like that on my section gang! And, ennyhow, they all take on like that when they're tarred of workin'!"

Oh, it was the same old thing.

All my life I've got my back up over something no more my business than the man in the moon; but seems to me when it's a matter of right or wrong, or good and bad, or the like, thinks I, there's no choice but to go to work and fight.

That blasted foreman infuriated me. And I can swear when I have to. Well, I set to and gave him such a dressing-down as you never heard.

I called him everything I ever heard, and then I made up some more pretty ones for good measure.

I told him I'd have him up before the nearest district territorial judge for criminal negligence. I told him I was a personal friend of John J. Summerdown, the president of the new railroad, and I'd, by God, have his job so fast he wouldn't know what hit him. I told him that anybody who'd stand by and let a man die instead of taking every chance there was to save him—I said was lower'n—anyway, you can't go through medical school without picking up a few fancy words.

He cocked his elbows and fists at me a couple of times. But when I'm right, I know I'm right, and that's all you need to handle a peasant like that.

He got scared, and we both wiped the sweat off our

brows at the same minute, the same gesture, and glared at each other, and I wondered if I looked as hot and messy and ignorant as he did, and I laughed.

The Mexicans were curious and asking questions and clawing at him. I turned around, like a nervous old maid, or a scared child, to see if the train was still there.

It had become a symbol of safety to me, the only way out of that yellow, yellow plain streaming with sunlight. Yes, it was still there, dusty black, and dusty white where the light rested.

The foreman talked to the men . . . there must have been about three dozen of them.

He may have been a fool but he was a crafty one.

He was talking in Mexican and telling them what I wanted to do to Pancho, their brother and friend. He pantomined surgery—knife in fist and slash and finger-scissors and then grab at belly, and then tongue out, and eyes rolled out of sight, and slump, and dead man; all this very intently, like a child doing a child's powerful ritual of play.

"Oh, yo, yo, yo," went all the Mexicans, and shook their fists at me, and showed their white teeth in rage. No sir, there'd be no cutting on Pancho!

"You see?" said the foreman. "I told 'em what you aim to do, and they won't have it."

I am no actor, and certainly no orator, but I turned to those poor peons and tried to show them as best I could how the only way to save Pancho, lying there like a baked peanut, was to operate right now.

The foreman kept up a kind of antiphony to my arguments.

You know? It was something like the old lyric struggle between good and evil—enlightenment and superstition.

There we were, miles from everything, on that plain

where the heat went up from the fried ground in sheets; nothing but a rickety line of tracks to keep us in the world, so to speak; and a struggle going on over the theory of life or death, as exemplified in the person of a perfectly anonymous wretch who'd eaten too many beans once too often!

I'd be damned if I'd quit.

I went back to the train and had more on my mind now than chivalry and Chaucer and Clouet.

She was still sitting there in her heavy starch and her yards and yards of black serge.

Her face was pink with heat and her glasses were a little moist. But she was like a calm and shady lake in that blistering wilderness, and her hands rested like ferns on the itchy plush of the seat which gave off a miniature dust storm of stifling scent whenever anything moved on it.

I could hear the argument and mutual reinforcement in cries and threats going on and gathering force out there in the little mob. It was like the manifest sound of some part of the day, the heat, the desert life, which being disturbed now filled the quavering air with protest.

When I stopped in the aisle beside her, she looked up sideways. Of course, she didn't mean it to, but it looked sly and humorous, and her glasses flashed.

"Excuse me, Sister," I said. "Have you ever had any hospital experience?"

"Is someone ill?"

Her voice was nearly doleful, but not because she was; no, it had the faintest trace of a German tone, and her words an echo of German accent, that soft, trolling, ach-Gott-im-Himmel charm that used to be the language of the old Germany, a comfortable sweetness that is gone now.

"There's a Mexican laborer out there who's doubled up

with appendicitis. I am a surgeon, by the way.''

"Yes, for a long time I was dietitian at Mount Mary Hospital, that's in Cleveland?''

"Well, you see what I think I ought to do.''

"So, you should operate?''

"It's the only thing't'd save him, and maybe that'll be too late.''

"Should we take him in the train and take care of him so? And operate when we reach town?''

Yes, you must see how placid she was, how instantly dedicated to the needs of the present, at the same time. She at once talked of what "we" had to do. She owned responsibility for everything that came into her life. I was young then, and I'm an old man now, but I still get the same kind of pride in doctors and those in holy orders when they're faced with something that has to be done for somebody else. The human value, mind you.

"I don't think they'll let us touch him. They're all Mexicans, and scared to death of surgery. You should've heard them out there a minute ago.''

"Yes, I hear them now.''

"What I think we'd better do is get to work right here. The poor wretch wouldn't last the ride to Eddy, God knows how long the train'd take.''

"But where, doctor!''

"Well, maybe one of those sheds.''

"So, and the train would wait?''

"Oh! I don't know. I can find out.''

I went and asked the conductor up in the next car. He said no, the train wouldn't wait, provided they ever got a chance to go.

"We'd have to take a chance on the train," I told Sister.

"Also, those men out there are not very nice about it. Maybe if you came out?"

At that she did hesitate a little; just a moment; probably the fraction it takes a celibate lady to adjust her apprehensions over the things she has heard about men, all of them, the very authors of sin, ancestors of misery, and custodians of the forbidden fruit of knowledge.

"It would have been more convenient," I said, "if I'd never got off the train. That groaning little animal would die, and when the train went, we'd be on it; but we cannot play innocent now. The Mexican means nothing to me. Life is not that personal to a doctor. But if there's a chance to save it, you have to do it, I suppose."

Her response to this was splendid. She flushed and gave me a terrific look, full of rebuke and annoyance at my flippancy. She gathered her great serge folds up in handfuls and went down the car walking angrily. I followed her and together we went over to the shed. The sunlight made her weep a little and blink.

The men were by now sweating with righteous fury. Their fascinating language clattered and threatened. Pancho was an unpleasant sight, sick and uncontrolled. The heat was unnerving. They saw me first and made a chorus. They then saw Sister and shut up in awe, and pulled their greasy hats off.

She knelt down by Pancho and examined him superficially and the flow of her figure, the fine robes kneeling in the dust full of ants, was like some vision to the Mexicans, in all the familiar terms of their Church. To me, it gave one of my infrequent glimpses into the nature of religious feeling.

She got up.

She turned to the foreman, and crossed her palms together. She was majestic and ageless, like any true authority.

"Doctor says there must be an operation on this man.
He is very sick. I am ready to help."

"W', lady," said the foreman, "you just try an' cut on
that Messican and see what happens!"

He ducked his head toward the laborers to explain this.

She turned to the men. Calmly, she fumbled for her long
rosary at her discipline and held up the large crucifix that
hung on its end. The men murmured and crossed themselves.

"Tell them what you have to do," she said to me coldly.
She was still angry at the way I'd spoken in the train.

"All right, foreman, translate for me. Sister is going to
assist me at an appendectomy. We'll move the man into
the larger shed over there. I'd be afraid to take him to
town, there isn't time. No: listen, this is better. What I will
do; we could move him into the train, and operate while
the train was standing still, and then let the train go ahead
after the operation is over. That way, we'd get him to town
for proper care!"

The foreman translated and pantomimed.

A threatening cry went up.

"They say you can't take Pancho off and cut on 'im on
the train. They want him here."

Everybody looked at Pancho. He was like a little monkey with eyes screwed shut and leaking tears.

The little corpus of man never loses its mystery, even to
a doctor, I suppose. What it is, we are; what we are, must
serve it; in anyone. My professor of surgery used to say,
"Hold back your pity till after the operation. You'll work

better and then the patient will be flattered to have it, and it might show up in the bill.''

"Very well, we'll operate here. Sister, are you willing to help me? It'll mean staying here till tomorrow's train.''

"*Ja*, doctor, of course.''

I turned to the foreman.

"Tell them.''

He shrugged and began to address them again.

They answered him, and he slapped his knee and h'yucked a kind of hound-dog laugh in his throat and said to us:

"W', if you go ahaid, these Messicans here say they'll sure 'nough kill you if you kill Pancho!''

Yes, it was worse than I could have suspected.

This was like being turned loose among savages.

You might have thought the searing heat of that light steel sky had got everybody into fanciful ways.

"Why, that's ridiculous!'' I said to him. "He's nearly dead now! Halsted himself might not save him! Nobody can ever guarantee an operation, but I can certainly guarantee that that man will die unless I take this one chance!''

"W', I dunno. See? That's what they said.''. . .

He waved at the Mexicans.

They were tough and growling.

Sister was waiting. Her face was still as wax.

"Can't you explain?'' I said.

"Man, you never can 'splain nothin' to this crew! You better take the church lady there, and just get back on that train; that's what you better do!''

Well, there it was.

"You go to hell!'' I said.

I looked at Sister. She nodded indignantly at me, and then smiled, sideways, that same sly look between her cheek and her lens, which she never meant that way; but from years of convent discretion she had come to perceive things obliquely and tell of them in whispers with many sibilants.

"Come on, we'll move him. Get some help there."

The Mexicans wouldn't budge. They stood in the way.

"Give me your pistol!"

The foreman handed it over. We soon got Pancho moved.

Sister helped me to carry him.

Sister was strong. I think she must have been a farm girl from one of the German communities of the Middle West somewhere. She knew how to work, the way to lift, where her hands would do the most good. Her heavy thick robes dragged in the dust. We went into the tool shed and it was like strolling into a furnace.

I hurried back to the train and got my bags and then went back again for hers. I never figured out how she could travel with so little and be so clean and comfortable. She had a box of food. It was conventional, in its odors, bananas, waxed paper, oranges, something spicy. Aside from that, she had a little canvas bag with web straps binding it. I wondered what, with so little allowed her, she had chosen out of all the desirable objects of the world to have with her and to own.

My instrument case had everything we needed, even to two bottles of chlorofrom.

I got back into the dusty red shed by flashing the foreman's pistol at the mob. Inside I gave it back to him through the window with an order to keep control over the peasants.

What they promised to do to me if Pancho died began to mean something, when I saw those faces, like clever dogs, like smooth-skinned apes, long-whiskered mice. I thought of having the conductor telegraph to some town and get help, soldiers or something; but that was nervously romantic.

It was dark in the shed, for there was only one window. The heat was almost smoky there, it was so dim. There was a dirt floor. We turned down two big tool cases on their sides and laid them together. They were not quite waist high. It was our operating table.

When we actually got started, then I saw how foolish it was to try it, without any hospital facilities. But I remembered again that it was this chance or death for the little Mexican. Beyond that, it was something of an ethical challenge. Yes, we went ahead.

I remember details, but now, so long after, maybe not in the right order.

I remember a particular odor, an oily smell of greasy sand, very powerful in the shed; the heat made the very dirt floor sweat these odors up, and they made me ill at ease in the stomach.

It was early afternoon. The sky was so still and changeless that it seemed to suspend life in a bowl of heat. The tin roof of the shed lowered a very garment of heat over us.

Faces clouded up at the window, to see, to threaten, to enjoy. We shook them away with the pistol. The foreman was standing in the doorway. Beyond him we had glimpses of the slow dancing silvery heat on the scratchy earth, and the diamond melt of light along the rails of the track.

The camp cook boiled a kettle of water.

Sister turned her back and produced some white rags from her petticoats.

She turned her heavy sleeves back and pinned her veils aside.

The invalid now decided to notice what was going on, and he tried to sit up and began to scream.

Sister flicked me a glance and at once began to govern him with the touch of her hands, and a flow of comforting melody in Deutsch noises. I got a syringe ready with morphine. And the mob appeared at the door, yelling and kicking up the stifling dust which drifted in and tasted bitter in the nose.

I shot the morphine and turned around.

I began to swear.

That's all I recall, not what I said. But I said plenty. Pancho yelled back at his friends who would rescue him. It was like a cat concert for a minute or so.

Then the morphine heavied the little man down again, and he fell silent.

Then I shut up, and got busy with the chloroform. Sister said she could handle that. It was suddenly very quiet.

My instruments were ready and we had his filthy rags off Pancho. Sister had an instinctive adroitness, though she had never had surgical experience. Yet her hospital service had given her a long awareness of the sometimes trying terms of healing. In fascinated silence we did what had to be done before the operation actually started.

There was a locust, or a cicada, some singing bug outside somewhere, just to make the day sound hotter.

The silence cracked.

"He is dead!" they cried outside.

A face looked in at the window.

Now the threats began again.

I said to the foreman:

"Damn you, get hold of that crowd and make them shut up! You tell them he isn't dead! You tell them—"

I began to talk his language again, very fancy and fast. It worked on him. I never cussed so hard in my life.

Then I turned back and I took up my knife.

There's a lot of dramatic nonsense in real life; for example: my hand was trembling like a wet dog, with that knife; but I came down near the incisionary area, and just before I made the first cut—steady? that hand got as steady as a stone!

I looked at Sister in that slice of a second, and she was biting her lips and staring hard at he knife. The sweat stood on her face and her face was bright red. Her light eyebrows were puckered. But she was ready.

In another second things were going fast.

I once told this story to someone, and later heard it repeated to someone else. I hardly recognized the events as my friend described them, because he made it all sound so dramatic and somehow like a scene in the opera, grand and full of high notes. No, it seems to me that the facts are more wonderful than all the things time and playgoing can do to a person's imagination. The whole situation couldn't have been meaner; more dangerous from forces like dirt and stupidity, instead of forces like fate or fascinating Mexican bandits. There was the hazard, too, of my own youth, my inexperience as a surgeon. There was my responsibility for Sister, in case any trouble might start. There was the heat and a patient with temperature and no way to cool off boiled water in a hurry, and the dust rising through the cracks of the door and window and walls of the shed as the outraged men kicked and shuffled outside. We could see the sheets of dusty light standing in the room's dusk, sliced from the gloom by a crack of that sunlight and its abstract splendor.

Oh, my surgery professor and my colleagues would've been shocked to see some of the things I did, and didn't do, that day!

I tried to hum a little tune instead of talk.

But now and then the noise outside would get worse.

Or the foreman would creak the door open and stick his varlet face in to peer.

Or the patient would almost swallow his tongue, making a noise like a hot sleeping baby.

So I'd swear.

Sister said nothing all the time.

She obeyed my instructions. Her face was pale, from so many things that she wasn't used to—the odors, the wound, manipulation of life with such means as knives and skill, the strain of seeing Pancho weaken gradually—she was glassy with perspiration. Her starched linen was melted. There was some intuitive machinery working between us. Aside from having to point occasionally at what I needed, things she didn't know the name of, I've never had a more able assistant at an operation in all my long life of practice.

I think it was because both she and I, in our professions, somehow belonged to a system of life which knew men and women at their most vulnerable, at times when they came face to face with the mysteries of the body and the soul, and could look no further, and needed help then.

Anyway, she showed no surprise. She showed none even at my skill, and I will admit that I looked at her now and then to see what she thought of my performance. For if I do say it myself, it was good.

She looked up only once, with a curious expression, and I thought it was like that of one of the early saints, in the paintings, her eyes filmed with some light of awareness and yet readiness, the hour before martyrdom; and this was when we heard the train start to go.

She looked regretful and forlorn, yet firm.

The engine let go with steam and then hooted with the exhaust, and the wheels ground along the hot tracks.

If I had a moment of despair, it was then; the same wavy feeling I'd had when the train had stopped here what seemed hours before.

The train receded in sound.

It died away in the plainy distance.

Shortly after, there was a rush of voices and cries and steps toward the shack.

It was the laborers again, many of whom had been put back to work on the track ahead of the engine, in order to let the train proceed. Now they were done. Now they were crazy with menace.

It was about four o'clock, I suppose.

Fortunately I was just finishing up. The door screeched in its shaken hinges and latch. I heard the foreman shouting at the men.

"Most Sacred Heart!" said Sister, on her breath, softly. It was a prayer, of course.

Then the door opened, and the foreman came in and closed it and leaned back on it.

He said they sent him in to see if Pancho were still living. I told him he was. He said he had to see. I said he was a blankety-blank meddling and low-down blank to come bothering me now; but that I was just done, and if he had to smell around he could come.

I showed him the pulse in the little old Mexican's neck, beating fast, and made him listen to the running rapid breath, like a dog's.

Then he looked around.

He was sickened, first, I suppose; then he got mad. The place was dreadful. There were unpleasant evidences of surgery around, and the heat was absolutely weakening, and the air was stifling with a clash of odors. Sister had gone to sit on a box in the corner, watching. She, too, must have looked like a challenge, an alien force, to him.

He grew infuriated again at the mysterious evidences of civilization.

He began to wave his gun and shout that the next time, by God, he'd fire on us, and not them Messicans out yander. He declared that he, too, was agin cuttin' on anybody. He was bewildered and sick to his stomach and suffering most of all from a fool's bafflement.

He bent down and tried to grab back the meager sheeting and the dressing on Pancho's abdomen. He was filthy beyond words. I butted him with my shoulder (to keep my hands away and reasonably clean) and he backed up and stood glaring and his mouth, which was heavy and thick, sagged and contracted in turn, like loose rubber.

Sister came forward and, without comment, knelt down by the wretched operating table which might yet be, for all I knew, a bier, and began to pray, in a rich whisper, full of hisses and soft impacts of r's upon her palate, and this act of hers brought some extraordinary power into the room; it was her own faith, of course, her own dedication to a simple alignment of life along two channels, one leading to good, the other to evil.

I was beginning to feel very tired.

I had the weakness after strain and the almost querulous relief at triumph over hazard.

I'd been thinking of her all along as a woman, in spite of her ascetic garb, for that was natural to me then. Now for the first time, listening to her pray, I was much touched, and saw that she was like a doctor who thinks enough of his own medicine to take some when he needs a lift.

The foreman felt it all, too, and what it did to him was to make him shamble sullenly out of the shed to join the enemy.

We watched all night.

It got hardly any cooler.

Late at night Sister opened her lunch box with little delicate movements and intentions of sociability, and made a little meal.

I felt intimate with her.

I had a sense of what, together, we had accomplished, and over and over I tried to feel her response to this. But none came. We talked rather freely of what we still had to do and whether we thought the Mexicans meant it, and whether the train crew knew what was going on, and if they'd report it when they reached Eddy.

We had an oil lamp that the foreman gave us.

When I'd get drowsy, my lids would drop and it seemed to me that the flame of the wick was going swiftly down and out; then I'd jerk awake and the flame would be going on steadily, adding yet another rich and melancholy odor to our little surgery.

I made Sister go to sleep, on her corner box, sitting with her back against the wall.

She slept in state, her hands folded, her body inarticulated under the volume of her robes, which in the dim lamplight looked like wonderful masses carved from some dark German wood by trolls of the Bavarian forest . . . so fancifully ran my mind through that vigil.

I saw morning come, like a cobweb, on the little window, then steal the whole sky that I could see; and then, just as a flavor of cool sweetness had begun to lift into the air off the plains, the sun appeared (rapidly, I thought; but then it was I, not the sun, whose fever hurried life along that day).

Early that day Pancho became conscious.

We talked to him and he answered.

He was inclosed in the mystery of pain and the relief of weakness.

When he identified Sister by her habit, he tried to cross

himself, and she smiled and crowed at him and made the sign of the Cross over him herself.

I examined him carefully, and he was all right. He had stood the shock amazingly well. It was too early for infection to show to any degree; but I began to have a certain optimism, a settling of the heart. It had come off. I began to think the day was cooler. You know: the sweetness over everything that seems to follow a feeling of honest satisfaction.

Then the crowd got busy again.

They saw Pancho through the window, his eyes open, his lips moving, smiling faintly and staring at Sister with a child's wonder toward some manifest loveliness hitherto known only in dream and legend.

In a second they were around at the door, and pushing in, babbling like children, crying his name aloud, and eager to get at him and kiss him and gabble and marvel and felicitate.

They were filthy and enthusiastic, flowing like life itself toward that which feeds it. They were, then, infection personified.

I shouted at them and made them stay back, I let them see Pancho, but from a distance of three feet.

He spoke to them, thinly; and they cried "Aiee!" with astonishment, and nodded their heads in homage. They couldn't have been more friendly now. They went yes-yes, and my-my, and how wonderful to have such a man! and he is my friend, and so forth.

But their very presence was dangerous, for they kicked up the dirt floor, and they hawked and spat on their words, and I finally put them out.

The foreman's mood was opposite to theirs.

He was now surly and disgruntled that we had pulled it off successfully.

He knew, as I had known, that the Mexicans really would kill if Pancho died.

We had the unpleasant impression that he felt cheated of a diverting spectacle.

We watched Pancho carefully all morning; he grew uncomfortable as the heat arose. But, then, so did we. It rose and rose, and the bugs sang; and the tin roof seemed to hum too, but that must have been dramatic inagination. I had all our plans made. When the noon train came along, we would flag it, and carefully move Pancho on board, and take him down the valley to Eddy, where he could spend two weeks in the company hospital.

Midmorning I stepped outside and called the men together and the foreman, and made them a speech. Now they had their hats off listening to me. Their little eyes could't have looked more kindly and earnest. *Sure,* I could take Pancho off on the train. *Sure,* they wanted him to get well. *By all means* the *señor médico* must do what he thought best. So, with a great show of love for them, I shook hands with myself at the little mob, feeling like a gifted politician.

The train finally arrived; and as it first showed, standing down the tracks in the wavering heat, it looked like a machine of rescue.

There was only one more thing there.

When we went to take Pancho on the train, the foreman refused to help.

"I won't he'p you," he declared. "I ain't got no authority t' move none of my men, and I won't he'p you."

I picked out two of the less earthy natives, and they

helped me to bring the patient on board the train. We carried him on a camp cot. It belonged to the foreman. When he saw that, he got so mad he threw down his hat and jumped on it. The dust flew. His fish-white brow broke into sweat. Then he came running to stop us. We barely got Pancho on the train in time, and the door closed and latched. It was a state of siege until the train went again. It must have been ten minutes. Fortunately I'd brought my bags on board the first thing, and Sister's.

We finally pulled out.

We looked out the rear window, and saw our desert hospital recede into the slow pulsing glassy air.

We could see the little figures, most of them waving.

Just at the last, one of them held forth his arm; and we saw a puff of smoke, and heard an explosion in our imaginations, and then heard the actual ring and sing-off of a bullet as it struck the rear of the car.

It was the foreman's farewell, the last, and futile, opinion of the ignorant.

The afternoon passed slowly in the train.

The heat and the dust were hard on everyone, and especially Pancho. I kept wetting down the cracks of the windows, and the doors, to keep the dust out if I could.

But soon the water was gone, and we had to sit there and hope.

We reached Eddy in the evening, and it was like a garden, after the endless plains and their sear life. We found green trees and artesian wells and cool fields of alfalfa.

There is little more to tell, and what there is, is not about Pancho, except that he made a recovery in the proper time.

It is about my saying goodbye to Sister.

It seemed to me we had been through a good deal together.

Now we were going to separate, for she was taking a stagecoach from Eddy on down into Texas somewhere, and I was going to stay a few days and see my patient out of the woods.

So we said goodbye in the lobby of the wooden hotel there, where she was going to spend the night.

Nobody knew what a good job I had done except Sister; and after we shook hands and I thanked her for her wonderful help, I waited a moment—just a little moment.

She knew I was nervous and tired; and it was vanity, of course, but I needed the little lift she could give me.

But she didn't say anything, while I waited; and then as I started to turn off and go, she did speak.

"I will pray for you, doctor."

"What?"

"That you may overcome your habit of profanity."

She bowed and smiled in genuine kindliness, and made her way to the stairs and disappeared.

Duty is an ideal and it has several interpretations, and these are likely to be closely involved with the character that makes them.

You might say that Sister and I represented life eternal and life temporal.

I never saw her again, of course; but if she's still alive, I have no doubt that she's one of the happiest people in the world.

THE BEES
by Joan Vatsek

One of the squat white candles on the makeshift altar flickered out. Every once in a while, the wind that whipped around the old farmhouse snapped in between the warped walls, and flattened the two flame-points. The altar was contrived of a few boards nailed together, and covered with a white cloth. On it, between the two candles, was a chalice and Bible, and nailed on the wall, a crucifix. These were provided by Father Amiens from the village when the convent was destroyed.

Sister Mary Emard, who was kneeling on the floor like the others, in front of a stiff-backed chair, got up heavily and relit the candle. She made a deep genuflection before the altar, lowering herself to her knees and bending her thick body forward. Then she got up and returned to her chair.

"*Ave Maria, gratia plena . . .*" the five nuns broke out in high, rapid chorus, as though the prayer were filled with a current that rushed them along, which they could neither stop nor slow down, but that rose of itself in irresistible continuity.

They made the sign of the cross at precisely the same moment, like soldiers, and sat up on the chairs for meditation, with their hands folded, and their heads slightly lowered. The common expression on all of their faces was one of complete detachment. It was as if they had suddenly gone out of the room, and it was empty, save that a hush as strong as a presence, had taken their place.

After a few minutes, as at a given signal, Mother Gervaise lifted her hands and held them, palm upward; the others followed her example. The hands of Mother Gervaise were short and powerful, her fingers about double the size one would expect them to be. As the loose sleeves of her habit fell away from them, they were almost startling.

"Blessed be God," began Mother Gervaise.

"Blessed be Jesus Christ," responded the four sisters.

Sister Mary Tomasina's voice dominated, clear and pure of tone. Sister Mary Tomasina had a kind of steel serenity, which nothing could alter or destroy. Mother Gervaise sometimes struggled with envy over this, for she herself was easily upset, and troubled with mild distempers. But in an emergency, Sister Tomasina stepped back, impersonal, while Mother rushed forward, and did what had to be done.

It was Mother Gervaise who had groped her way between the toppling walls, calling, "Sisters! Sisters! This way!" She who had shaken the blubbering, terrified Sister Emard back to normal, and who had sent Sister Therese running to the village for help.

Mother Gervaise lowered her hands. The five women rose, and filed out from the room which they had set apart for their chapel, falling in line one after the other, as though there were still twenty of them. They went into the kitchen, the only warm spot in the farmhouse, which belonged to Sister Therese's brother, away now in the army.

Sister Mary Emard came back a moment after, blew out the precious candles, patted the altar cloth, straightened the chairs. She was a lay sister, and was troubled chiefly by her lack of customary menial tasks, for after cleaning and airing and cooking the meals, there was no work for her to do. She thought, heavily, of the day that was only half-done: without bustle, without floors to sweep, groceries to be bought, farmhands to scold.

The convent had hummed, what with the school and the farm work to oversee. There was a sizeable patch of land, enough to provide for the needs of the sisters, with a little over for profit. They had raised the best vegetables in the countryside, and had the best honey. They had kept chickens, a few cows, and two big horses that could be hitched to the plough. Since the war, to be sure, much of the land lay unworked.

But still, their ordered community existence had continued. Now that it was swept away, the remaining sisters did not know how to take hold of life again. That was why they stayed on, in the first shelter they had thought of, unwilling to leave for the city and join the others of their order in the mother house. Mother Gervaise put off departure day after day, and two weeks passed in this way.

She tried to find excuse in the fact that they rigidly kept their rules. Every morning they went to the village to hear Mass, they did what work they could find, and they did not relax discipline at meals, but ate in silence, as always, except on feast days.

When Sister Emard went back to the kitchen, Mother Gervaise was ready to begin grace. Slowly, with no pleasure, they ate the meal that Emard had prepared for them. She did not blame them, for it was not seemly to enjoy anything at such a time, and yet, in a way, she resented it. She had bent over the old kitchen stove and grown as heated over it as over the good one in the big clean convent kitchen. She had put as much love into cooking the spinach and potatoes, as chicken and cake on great holidays. Then the sisters were allowed to speak, and after a High

Mass, vibrant with music and the smell of flowers, they had tumbled laughingly into the dining room, as though just returning from a journey with a friend.

After they finished eating, Sister Mary Therese rose and began to gather up the plates. She was longing for something to do. Her young face, with the one troubled crease in the forehead, a crease that appeared and deepened whenever she had any feeling of guilt about what she had done or not done, was there now, whenever Mother Gervaise looked at her. She was the youngest and somehow the dearest of the nuns who had been left to her, for as a child she had come to the convent to school and had grown up in it.

Sister Mary Emard got up at once, crossly. "I can do the dishes," she said.

"Let me wipe them!" said Sister Therese. She looked at Mother Gervaise, as though asking for a favor.

"All right," said the Mother Superior, nodding, and giving the lay sister a little glance of reproof. The two of them began to clear away, Sister Emard still a little resentful of having to share her tasks.

Sister Mary Tomasina rose in her untroubled way and went to a cupboard against the wall, which was intended for dishes, but where the sisters now kept the few belongings salvaged from the wreck, and some things donated by the villagers.

Only once had Mother Gervaise and Sister Tomasina gone back to the convent. One wing was still recognizable; it was there that the five of them had been when the bomb fell and the rest of the building collapsed, crashing.

Besides the table, the cupboards, the chairs and stove, there was a pile of kindling wood in one corner of the kitchen. They watched this pile diminishing, as though it were an hourglass, knowing certainly that when it disappeared, they must go.

On the bleak wooden walls were three holy pictures, two of which Father Amiens had given them, and one which Sister Tomasina had found in the ruins. This last was of Mary, and the edge of it was charred. They all looked on it with special reverence, and were grateful to Tomasina for the way she had tacked it up, with unemphasized solemnity.

Little Sister Mary Elizabeth sat quite still at the table, with her bright brown eyes in her pale face, following Sister Tomasina's movements. There was a flowing rhythm in the older sister's walk, in everything she did, even in the way she took up the sewing she had begun the night before and sat down with it at the table. She was mending a nun's habit, turning the frayed sleeves. Sister Elizabeth was soothed by watching her.

She herself was slight and high-strung, and had been frequently ill. It was during a fever, when she was only about eleven years old, that she had seen a vision of which she rarely spoke, and it was then that she had made up her mind to become a nun. She had accepted her probable early death, with a kind of grave sweetness, long ago, and her conviction of it was catching.

All of a sudden, on one of her quick and birdlike impulses, the young sister got up and whispered something to Mother Gervaise.

"I don't think you'll find anything," said the Mother gently, "but try."

So Sister Elizabeth put a knitted shawl around her narrow shoulders, and opened the door. As she did so, a blast of rushing autumn wind swept into the kitchen and seemed about to toss her back, but she stood poised, with the door held open, her frail body opposing the blustering force. She went out, drawing the door shut.

Mother Gervaise took a chair and sat down by the window. There was something startling in her just sitting like that. The sisters always thought of her as inspired with tireless, creative energy. Young Sister Therese glanced at her, rag poised in her hand, with a look almost of fear.

"Aren't you well, Mother?" she asked.

"Oh, I am all right, child," answered Mother Gervaise.

She looked out at the gray day. The bare earth was caked and hard, running in long bleak furrows from the farmhouse to the road.

"Your brother tilled the fields before he left," she remarked, noting it for the first time consciously.

"Yes," said Sister Therese. "That was last year, when the war broke out." She thought of her brother, probably throwing bombs too, and a fierce pain set her praying in his stead.

"Sister Tomasina," said Mother suddenly, as if it had been pressing on her mind for some time, "did you notice that our beehives were untouched?"

"Yes, Mother, I noticed that," said Sister Tomasina, stitching steadily.

"Don't you think we should see to them for the winter?" she asked. There was an odd quality of appeal in the older woman's voice. She was asking for help, in some indefinable loss. Therese heard it, and felt suddenly dismayed, as though a pillar were swaying, toppling. Sister Emard swished the water loudly, as though to drown out the sound.

It had happened once or twice, in their long years together, that Mother Gervaise had needed Sister Tomasina badly, Tomasina's steady fervor, like white heat, which she gave out to those around her, that one could feel when she entered the room, and that increased when called upon. She seemed to radiate it now, without even looking up.

"Why not, Mother?" she assented quietly.

"The drones will eat all the honey," she explained, with a gesture of one short, argumentative hand. "The bees will become wild," she added, as though this disturbed her very much.

The thought of the bees worried her. It did not seem right to leave them deserted there, with winter coming on. The bees had been her special hobby and care; she was able to thrust among them cleverly without being stung. Sister Tomasina had once said that she spent more time with her bees than with the sisters, and that she was fonder of being in the fields than in the classroom. It was a reproach that Mother Gervaise had not forgotten, for it was partially deserved.

The door was pushed open, and Sister Elizabeth came in, her thin, small face pink from the wind. In her hands she held, carefully, a little bunch of red leaves.

"You see, Mother!" she exclaimed. "I did find something! There was just this clump left on one of the bushes. They are almost as good as flowers."

"Let me see!" cried Sister Therese, as though there were at least a dozen sisters around, all pushing to see.

"Oh, they are lovely!" she cried, and the two young nuns bent over the red leaves with unfeigned delight.

"Put them in water," bade Sister Tomasina in her calm. cool voice, smiling at their pleasure.

"Yes," said Therese, "bring them here, Elizabeth!"

She eagerly worked up and down on the handle of the old-fashioned pump.

They hung up the leaves in a little glass vial under the charred picture of Mary. The bit of color there cheered them all.

"Are you going to the beehives today, Mother?" asked Sister Emard, hesitantly. She had picked up a rag and was polishing the worn kitchen table.

"You don't mind going?" asked Mother sharply. The sisters had at first refused to go back to the convent, all except Tomasina.

In her restlessness for occupation, Sister Emard had half forgotten that it meant seeing the ruins of their beloved convent. Her round, simple peasant face contracted and she straightened for a minute, her heavily planted body trembling a little with consternation.

"No, Mother," she answered at last. "I don't mind going. That is," she amended conscientiously, "I will go." She began to rub the table again, with desperate vigor.

"Then let us go at once," said Mother Gervaise, feeling that a general decision had been reached, and that if the lay sister was willing, the others would certainly not withdraw.

"We must see to the bees," explained Tomasina to little Sister Elizabeth, folding up her sewing.

Elizabeth looked puzzled. " But we are going to the city soon," she said, "aren't we?" She turned her bright brown eyes on the Mother Superior's face.

"Yes—yes," Mother Gervaise hesitated, "but still, they will be here in the spring. We can come down, perhaps, to get the honey. If it is not stolen," she added.

Or bombed, thought little Sister Elizabeth, or bombed. But who would want to bomb a beehive? There is no sense to that, she thought. The bees do nobody harm. They hum and work and gather honey, and by and by they die.

"The beehives will be there when my brother returns,"

said Sister Therese loudly, as though someone were deaf, her forehead wrinkling with emphasis. "He will surely go to the convent, and they will be there, at least." The idea comforted her, as though the war were already over, and he were coming home.

"We had better take rags," said Mother, organizing, in her old way, "to wrap around our hands. I don't think the bees will mind, though, they know us too well. Sister Elizabeth, take your shawl."

"Yes, Mother."

"Sister Emard, lock the back door."

"Yes, Mother."

They went out, locking the front door also. There was nothing in the old farmhouse that anyone would want, but the habit of locking possessions entrusted to them, though not theirs, was too strong to be broken.

The wind caught up their garments like billowing black sails, and blew out the long draperies at the back. There was a smell of frost in the air, the deeply penetrating tang before winter, and it rushed through their lungs with a mighty, tearing zest.

Suddenly Sister Therese felt so glad to be alive, breathing the strong sharp air, that she had to do something joyful and carefree. She was close to her childhood, especially here, on the very land where she had raced her brother many times.

"You're It!" she cried exultantly, tagging Mary Elizabeth, and fleeing ahead of her. The slim Elizabeth ran gamely after her, but started panting almost at once, her thin cheeks pink in an instant.

"Sisters!" exclaimed Sister Tomasina. She was really shocked. She could not forget for an instant, the terrible happenings of two weeks ago.

"Let them be," said Mother Gervaise. "Let them laugh a little."

But she could feel Tomasina's silent disapproval, like a visible, shining sword between them. The two women walked along side by side, Sister Emard a little behind them, respectfully.

Their hard boots crunched on the caked autumn earth.

Far away there were a series of sudden explosions, like haphazard thunder.

Therese and Elizabeth stopped, and looked back questioningly. They waited, grown quiet, and walked along beside Mother Gervaise.

"They must be bombing again, in the city," said Tomasina, sternly serene as ever.

They came to the road and stamped their feet, shaking off the earth. Nobody answered Tomasina's remark. They set off toward the bend that would bring them in sight of the convent.

"I wonder if they will fly back this way again," went on Tomasina deliberately. She was convinced that fear, if expressed, lost some of the power it possessed when kept in secret.

"We are needed, in the city," she said next, with seeming irrelevance. But they all understood her. She thought that they were shirking: remaining, bound by their nostalgia, near the spot where the other sisters had been, with such expert aim, so dreadfully annihilated. They wanted to keep vigil a little longer, to alleviate the suddenness of their death.

"Yes, yes, Sister," said Mother Gervaise hurriedly, "yes, we will go soon now. Any day, now. Tomorrow, perhaps. We are of no use here. There are nurses needed, as you say. Or didn't you say? At any rate, it is true."

Mother Gervaise was not in the habit of expressing herself so disjointedly, in fact, it was disconcerting to hear her ramble on in such a manner. She frowned, and stepped out briskly, her hands clenched into two round, determined fists.

"It *is* true," admitted Sister Therese, the little line in her forehead like a furrow now, "only . . ."

She hated to go to a strange place, where not Mother Gervaise, but someone else, would be the Superior. She hated to go further away from the convent to which she had gone to school. She remembered vividly when she was first taken to Mother Gervaise, rather awed, and how Mother got up from her work at the desk, and talked to her, smiling down, and how at the end she laid one strong, light hand on her small head in blessing.

"Only what?" asked Sister Tomasina, and this time Therese was aware of that bright shining sword between the unfaltering sister and the world.

"Only it is hard to go away," finished Therese.

"There are much harder things than that," reproved Tomasina, "happening every day."

They turned the bend in the road that they had all been dreading. But the looming thing across the fields seemed less dramatic in the gray daylight than the picture each one had of the flaming, falling mass.

It was not far to the convent, across the fields. Sister Therese had often run all the way when she was late to school, walking forgetfully along the road, till suddenly she caught sight of it standing there, waiting for her.

The five nuns walked along with regimented step, saying nothing.

When they came quite near to the charred black remains, and the splintered rafters sticking out crazily, Sister

Mary Emard fell back still further and made the sign of the cross several times in quick succession.

"Santa Maria," she whimpered. Terror came upon her again, and she imagined wildly that she could hear the sisters screaming as the bomb came down, inexplicably, from heaven.

"Hush, Sister," said Mother Gervaise.

But the five women came to a stop. The wind whipped their garments about them, so that their bodies looked like the wrapped bodies of insects, cocooned and caught. They gazed at the wreck of their home, thinking of the sisters who had been their companions, and who had met death so suddenly, without a moment to compose themselves into courage and dignity.

"It's all that's left," thought Mother Gervaise dully. She had been Superior of the convent for more than twenty years.

Little Sister Mary Elizabeth sighed. Her face was pale again. She shivered, and drew the knitted shawl more closely about her.

"We should not have brought you, child," said Mother Gervaise contritely.

"But I could not have stayed alone!" she exclaimed.

"No, to be sure," said Mother, "to be sure." And they all murmured that certainly she could not have stayed alone, to quench the sudden panic in her brown eyes.

"Come," said Mother Gervaise.

The beehives were around at the back. They threaded the ruined building, and their feet came across a piece of blackened wood now and again. There were a dozen hives.

A look of pleasure came to the Mother's face. She went to the first hive and opened it. The bees were huddled together in little clusters, clinging to the walls, heavy with sleep. She picked out the drones, carefully, taking them up with delicate skill between her thick thumb and forefinger. Throwing them down on the earth, she trampled on them.

Sister Tomasina went to the next hive. Soon they were all working. Every once in a while Sister Therese cried out childishly that she was stung, and paused to suck at her finger, but nobody paid much attention. They were all stung several times, except Mother, in spite of the rags they wrapped about their hands and the sleepy laziness of the bees.

"Now let's see," said Mother Gervaise, walking from one hive to the other, her sharp eyes on the lookout for the useless drones that still remained.

"Fine," she said. "Now we must cover the beehives, or they will certainly freeze. This winter will be a hard winter." She began to wrap rags around the beehives.

"There is straw left in the barn," said Sister Tomasina, "some of it is black, but we could use it."

"Will you go and get it then, Sister?"

"Come with me, Emard," said Tomasina. She chose the lay sister because she considered it wrong that she should be so superstitious about going inside the charred buildings.

She led the way, and went into the partly shattered barn, lowering her head slightly. She began to gather up straw in her skirt, her tall form bending rhythimically. Sister Emard panted after her, chattering half to herself, "Santa Maria! Santa Maria!"

They carried the straw back and made two trips more, while the others padded the hives with it.

"The bombing has stopped," remarked Tomasina, after a time.

"So it has!" exclaimed Therese in surprise. "I forgot all about it, working."

"Yes," chimed in little Sister Elizabeth, straightening her narrow shoulders.

They all agreed that they had not even noticed it for the last two hours. They had enjoyed the communion of working together. They felt restored, whole once more. The little sisterhood breathed again as a unit. Mother's face, that had aged so remarkably in the last two weeks, was smoothed out.

"There," she said with deep satisfaction, when they had finished, as though this act of preparing the bees for the winter had implications for her especially, which could not be explained.

The little group drew together. The wind buffeted their garments, tugging at their veils. It whipped through the ruined convent, whistling around the rafters.

"Now we can go," she said. They knew she did not mean that they could return to the farm.

Quiet fell upon them suddenly, at the thought of really leaving, perhaps forever. They stood in the attitude of listening, as though waiting unconsciously for the bombing to burst out again. But they were waiting for something else, for something more from Mother Gervaise, who guided and directed them, who had taught them and disciplined them with such infallible instinct. They looked to her to express what was in their hearts, to assure them of purpose, and lessen the pain of farewell.

"Yes," she repeated decisively, to leave them in no doubt as to what they must face, and then—"we will go tomorrow, to the city."

The frail Mary Elizabeth looked down, and crossed her slender fingers as in prayer.

"We should start early," said Tomasina, in her clear, uncompromising tones, "early in the morning, Mother." She stood straight and tall, ready for service.

Sister Emard said nothing, she moved her head a little, this way and that, as though she had a halter round her neck. Her heavy face wore a faint, half-comprehending smile.

And still they stood there, unwilling to break the last of their moments with the memories that haunted them, of the familier and the safe.

"They will live through the winter," said Mother softly, reflectively.

Then she held out her hands toward them, enfolding them and the beehives behind them, in a gesture of completion, with that rare and profound tenderness for which they loved her.

"Yes," cried out Therese, starting forward and grasping her hand with a sob, "We will live through the winter!"

And suddenly they were all of them laughing and crying, and running across the field, running from the past, to the busy and immediate present.

MEDITATION
by Katharine West

She was old, very old. (She called it seasoned.) She was gnarled. (She called it weathered.) She had gone back to wearing the centuries-old black habit. Not because the tradition appealed to her, but because it was warmer and swirled about her legs, hiding her bulging, varicose veins.

She knelt now, leaning back a bit, at Mass in the convent chapel. Around her were the other nuns, most of them in their hospital whites. Competent women, a strange mixture of dedication and ambition. Wedded to the idea that their way of life was the best. On some, she could see, making a bright Turner-like splash against the white, the emblematic red roses of the Right-to-Life Movement.

The chapel's temperature was comfortable. A truce had been reached in the "War of the Windows," a heavy battle between two camps, "the Openers" and "the Closers." She sided with neither. She considered the Openers, like the Carter-Baptists, to be literalists (and probably menopausal). They were, she asserted, literal followers of Good Pope John opening wide the windows. Only his purpose had been to let in a fresh breeze. What the Openers let in was generally a winter gale. Yet the Closers were no better. The windows that they kept closing, in her opinion, were often a reflection of their lives, an attempt to shut out the world.

She looked upon herself as a neutral in this fray. At times she wondered if her whole life had not been that of a neutral, or more accurately, a middle-of-the-roader. The *via media* of St. Thomas Aquinas. The Miltonic concept of not too much.

She relished the way her thoughts wandered in chapel. She regarded it as stream-of-consciousness which brought therapeutic purging. It left her with no bitterness. True, she did at times feel disdain, but she felt gratitude as well. Sometimes she thought she would have been a better person in a different way of life. She was tolerant of everyone except her fellow sisters.

It was especially during the preaching that her thoughts roamed. She knew that she had set opinions about sermons, today called homilies. She remembered a Protestant scholar claiming that one of Luther's important contributions was improving the sermon. In that case, she mused, the world today could use another Luther. Yes, she recognized her feelings were strong about sermons, their length and content. She wanted them short and meaty. She had never been able to figure out how poor preachers (for this, read the Verbal Majority) could be unaware of their mediocrity. And perhaps they weren't! On the other hand, she recalled reading in Nietzsche that the mediocre find their happiness in mediocrity. She considered it a pleasantly snobbish insight.

She thought of her brother, the priest, junior by ten years. His sermons were still very good, in fact, excellent—brief, substantive, enthusiastic. They always had been, even when he was a young priest, although in early days she worried that he might posses a certain stuffiness. She remembered the day after his ordination. Someone in the family had asked him, "What shall we call you now?" Benignly he had replied, "Just call me Father Jim." All that stuffiness, if that was what it had been, fortunately was lost years ago. Strong in his faith, he had no need of pretense.

The Mass was moving toward the kiss of peace, a Rotar-
ianesque handshake. She thought how much she had once
liked the gesture, its warmth, its spontaneity. She had even
seen it transform people at least for a few seconds. Now
she knew that there were some sisters with whom she
would rather not shake hands. One of these often sat near
her. She would not refuse to shake her hand. She had had
to find a way to handle the awkwardness. At first, she recalled, she had tried extending limp, impersonal fingers.
She had felt, however, that this was a betrayal of her resolute nature. She was satisifed with her present method
which was to extend her hand as though she were a chate-
laine greeting a inferior. Always she said "Mercy" to this
particular nun, never "Peace."

An old question once again crossed her mind: What had
caused her to go to the convent? In the past, many had
asked her this. It was not an easy question to answer. Put
simply, she thought it was how God wished her to spend
her life. Now, looking back, she wondered if that were not
an arrogant assumption. Yet she would not say that she re-
gretted her decision. Her trust in Providence was too
strong for that.

When the Great Exodus of sisters began in the latter half
of the Sixties and in the Seventies she gave no thought to
leaving, although she wondered what she might have done
had she been a younger woman. She liked to think that it
would have made no difference. She thought of Sartre's
No Exit and his definition of hell. "Hell is—other
people!" Perceptive, even if a bit extreme. She chuckled.
One might think he had lived in a convent or monastery
rather than with Simone de Beauvoir all those long years.
She caught herself up. No, she admitted, that was not fair

to sisters in their convents. What had St. Augustine said? Never had he met better men and never worse in the monastery.

She wondered what lay ahead; what further changes in convent life there might be. Community—whatever that meant—seemed to be the most-talked-about value. Certainly one thing community did mean was that the sisters took care of their own. For this she felt a detached gratitude. She thought of an observation she had recently read in Auchincloss' newest book (thank God she could still read without difficulty, no need yet for big-print editions). The central character asked himself if "people" had not replaced "individuals" in the heart of his wife, a tireless reformer, and he queried further if this were not perhaps the rather unlovable characteristic of saints. She would not say that in the convent people had been substituted for individuals. The individual mattered.

About her she heard a rustle. The sisters were leaving the chapel. Mass was over. She came to with a start. She had missed Holy Communion. Never before had this happened to her.

THE LORD'S DAY
by J. F. Powers

The trees had the bad luck to be born mulberry and to
attract bees. It is not the first time, Father said, and so you
could not say he was being unfair. It was, in fact, the second time that a bee had come up and stung him on the
front porch. What if it had been a wasp? How did he know
it was one of the mulberry bees? He knew. That was all.
And now, Sister, if you'll just take the others into the
house with you, we'll get down to work. She had ordered
the others into the convent, but had stayed to plead pri-
vately for the trees. The three big ones must go. He would
spare the small one until such time as it grew up and became a menace.

Adjusting the shade, which let the sun through in with-
ered cracks like the rivers on a map, she peeked out at the
baking schoolyard, at the three trees. Waves of heat wandered thirstily over the pebbles, led around by the uncertain wind. She could see the figure of Father walking the
heat waves, a fat vision in black returning to the scene of
the crime, grabbing the axe away from the janitor. . . .
Here, John, let me give her the first lick! . . . And so,
possibly fancying himself a hundred years back, the most
notable person at the birth of a canal or railroad, and with
the children for his amazed audience, he had dealt the first
blow. Incredible priest!

She left the room and went downstairs. They were waiting in the parlor. She knew at a glance that one was missing. Besides herself, they were twelve—the apostles. It was
the kind of joke they could appreciate, but not to be carried too far, for then one of them must be Judas, which

55

was not funny. In the same way she, as the leader of the apostles, feared the implication as blasphemous. It was not a very good joke for the convent, but it was fine to tell lay people, to let them know there was life there.

She entered the little chapel off the parlor. She knelt for a moment and then, genuflecting in the easy, jointless way that comes from years of it, she left. Sister Eleanor, the one missing, followed her into the parlor.

"All right, Sisters, let's go." She led them through the sagging house, which daily surpassed itself in gloominess and was only too clean and crowded not to seem haunted, and over the splintery floor rising and sinking underfoot like a raft. She opened the back door and waited for them to pass. She thought of herself as a turnkey releasing them briefly to the sun and then to their common, sudden doom. They proceeded silently across the schoolyard, past the stumps bleeding sap, the bright chips dirtying in the gravel, a few twigs folded in death.

Going under the basketball standards she thought they needed only a raven or two to become gibbets in the burning sun. A pebble lit in the lacings of her shoe. She stopped to free it. She believed she preferred honest dust to manufactured pebbles. Dust lent itself to philosophizing and was easier on the children's knees.

They climbed the cement steps, parting the dish towels on the porch as portieres, and entered the rectory. The towels were dry and the housekeeper would be gone. She sensed a little longing circulate among the sisters as they filed into the kitchen. It was all modern, the *after* for the *before* they would always have at the convent. She did not care for it, however. It hurt the eyes, like a field of sunny snow. A cockroach turned around and ran the other way on the sink. At least he was not modern.

The dining room was still groggy from Sunday dinner. They drew chairs up to the table in which the housekeeper had inserted extra leaves before taking the afternoon off. The table was covered with the soiled cloth that two of them would be washing tomorrow. They sighed. There in the middle of the table, in canvas sacks the size of mail-bags, were the day's three collections, the ledgers and index cards for recording individual contributions. They sat down to count.

With them all sitting around the table, it seemed the time for her to pray, "Bless us, O Lord, and these Thy gifts . . ."

Sister Antonia, her assistant, seized one of the sacks and emptied it out on the table. "Come on, you money-changers, dig in!" Sister Antonia rammed her red hands into the pile and leveled it off. "Money, money, money."

"Shall we do what we did last week?" asked Sister Florence. She looked hopefully at Sister Antonia.

"Cubs and White Sox?" said Sister Antonia. "O.K., if it'll make you happy." Sister Antonia dumped out the other sack. The winner would be the one counting the most money. They chose up sides and changed seats accordingly, leaving Sister Antonia and herself to do the envelopes.

Sister Louise and Sister Paula, who could remember several regimes before hers and might have been mothers superior themselves, constituted a resistance movement, each in her fashion. Sister Louise went to sleep in a nice, unobtrusive way, chin in wimple. But Sister Paula—Sister Cigar Box to the children, with whom she was *not* a great favorite—stayed awake to grumble and would touch only the coins that appeared old, foreign, or very new to her. She stared long and hard at them while Sister Louise dozed with a handful of sweaty nickels.

It was their way of informing everyone of their disapproval, of letting her know it had not been like this in former times, that Sunday had been a day of rest under other leadership. They were right, she knew too well, and was ashamed that she could not bring herself to make a stand against Father. Fortunately, the two old sisters could not carry the resistance beyond themselves. She left them to Sister Antonia. The others, to make the contest even, divided the dead weight between them. The Cubs got Sister Louise and Sister Paula went with the White Sox.

A horn tooted out in front of the rectory, and from his room upstairs young Father shouted, *"Cominnggg!* Tell him I'm coming!" The shout sailed down the stairway and out to Father on the porch.

"He's coming," Father called to the car. "How's your health?"

She could not catch the reply for the noise young Father made running around upstairs. He had on his shower clogs and was such a heavy man.

Finally the ceiling settled, and young Father came clattering down the front stairs, dragging his golf clubs behind him. He spoke to Father on the porch.

"Want me home for Devotions, Father?"

"Oh hell, Bill, have a good time. Won't anybody come in weather like this but the nuns. I'll handle it."

"Well—thanks, Boss."

"Look out for that nineteenth hole; that's all I got to say. Have a good time."

"You talked me into it."

Sister Cigar Box dropped a half dollar from an unnecessary height and listened to the ring. "Lead! And I suppose that was that Father O'Mammon in his new machine out waking the dead! I'm on to him. I had him in school."

"O'Hannon, Sister," corrected Sister Antonia.

Of St. Judas's parish. I know."

"Of St. Jude's, Sister."

"Crazy!"

Father's radio woke up with a roar.

"The symphony!" breathed Sister Charlotte, who gave piano lessons to beginners six days a week.

"It's nice," Sister Cigar Box rasped when Father dialed away from it. *"Wasn't* it?"

Now Father was getting the news and disputing with the commentator. "Like hell you say!" Father had the last word and strode into the dining room with his collar off, bristling.

"Good afternoon, Father!" they all sang out.

"We'll have to fight Russia," he said, plunging into the kitchen. She heard him in the refrigerator and could tell that, rather than move things, he squeezed them out. He passed through the dining room, carrying a bottle of beer and a glass.

"Hot," he said to nobody.

The radio came on again. Father listened to an inning of the ball game. "Cubs are still in second place!" he shouted back to them.

"Thank you, Father," said Sister Florence involuntarily.

Sister Cigar Box said, "Humph!"

Now she could tell from the scraping noises that Father was playing himself a game of checkers. Periodically the moves became more rapid, frenzied, then triumphant. He was winning every game.

She asked Sister Eleanor how the map was coming.

"All in except Rhode Island and Tennessee. I don't know what's keeping them." They all knew Sister Eleanor

was putting together a map from free road maps she got
from the oil companies. She had been unable to get an ap-
propriation from Father for a new one. He said they had a
map already and that he had seen it a few years back. She
had tried to tell him it was too old and blurry, that Arizona
and Oklahoma, for instance, had now been admitted to the
Union. Who cares about them? said Father. Give the kids
a general idea—that's all you can do in the grades. Same as
you give them catechism. You'd have them all studying
Saint Thomas in the Latin.

"How big's it now?" asked Sister Antonia.

"Enormous. We'll have to put it up in sections, I guess.
Like the Eastern states, the Middle Atlantic, and so on."

"You could hang it in the gym."

"If Father moved out his workshop."

"Some of the maps don't dovetail when they come from
different companies. But you get detail you wouldn't get in
a regular map. It's just awkward this way."

Father appeared in the door of the dining room. "How's
she look?"

"More envelopes this week, Father," said Sister Antonia.

"Guess that last blast got them. How's the hardware department?"

Three sisters saw each other about to speak, gulped, and
said nothing. "It's better, isn't it, Sisters?" inquired Sister
Antonia.

"Yes, Sister."

Father came over to the table. "What's this?" He
picked up a Chinese coin with a hole in it that Sister
Cigar Box had been glad to see earlier. "Well, we don't get
so many buttons nowadays, do we?" Father's fingers
prowled the money pile sensitively.

"No, Father," said Sister Florence. "One last week, one today." She looked like a small girl who's just spoken her piece.

"One again, huh? Have to tell the ushers to bear down. Here, Sister, you keep this." Father gave the Chinese coin to Sister Cigar Box. "For when you go on the missions."

Sister Cigar Box took the coin from him and said nothing—about the only one not smiling—and put it down a trifle hard on the table.

Father went over to the buffet. "Like apples? Who wants an apple?" He apparently expected them to raise their hands but did not seem disappointed when no one did. He placed the bowl on the table for them. Three apples on top were real, but the ones underneath were wax and appeared more edible. No one took an apple.

"Don't be bashful," Father said, straying into the kitchen.

She heard him in the refrigerator again.

In a moment he came out of the kitchen with a bottle of beer and a fresh glass, passed quickly through the room, and, hesitating at the door, turned toward them. "Hot weather," he said. "Makes you sleepy. That's all I got to say." He left them for the porch.

The radio went on again. He had the Catholic Hour for about a minute. "Bum speaker," he explained while dialing. "Else I'd keep it on. I'll try to get it for you next week. They're starting a new series."

"Yes, Father," said Sister Florence, not loud enough to be heard beyond the table.

Sister Cigar Box said, "Humph!"

Father could be heard pouring the beer.

Next he got "The Adventures of Phobe Smith, the

Phantom Psychiatrist." It was better than the ball game and news.

But Phobe, if Muller wasn't killed in the plane crash and Mex was really working for British Intelligence, tell me how the heck could Colonel Barnett be a Jap spy and still look like—uh—the real Colonel Barnett? Plastic surgery. Plastic surgery—well, I never! Plus faricasalicasuki. Plus farica—what! Faricasalicasuki—a concentrate, something like our penicillin. And you knew all the time——! That Colonel Barnett's wife, Darlene, was not. . . unfaithful? Yes! I'm afraid so. Whew!

An organ intervened and Father turned off the radio.

She recorded the last contribution on the last index card. The money was all counted and wrapped in rolls for the bank. The White Sox had won. She told them to wait for her and ventured out on the porch, determined to make up for the afternoon, to show them that she knew, perhaps, what she was doing.

"Father"—he was resting in an orange-and-green deck chair—"I wonder if you could come and look at our stove."

Father pried his legs sideways, sat up, and rubbed his eyes. "Today? *Now?*"

She nodded dumbly and forced herself to go through with it. "It's smoking so we can't use it at all." She was ready, if necessary, to mention the old sisters who were used to hot tea.

Father massaged his bald head to rouse himself. He wrinkled the mottled scalp between his hands and it seemed to make a nasty face at her. "Let's go," he said. Evidently he had decided to be peppy—an example to her in time of adversity. He scooped his collar off the radio and let it snap to around his neck. He left it that way, unfastened.

"Father is going to look at the stove," she told them in the dining room. They murmured with pleasure.

Father went first, a little unsteady on stiff legs, not waiting for them. He passed the stumps in the yard with satisfaction, she thought. "Whyn't you ask John to look at it yesterday?" he demanded over his shoulder.

She tried to gain a step on him, but he was going too fast, wobbling in a straight line like a runaway trolley. "I thought you'd know more about it, Father," she lied, ashamed that the others could hear. John, looking at it, had shaken his head.

"Do we need a new one, John?"

"If you need a stove, Sister, you need a new one."

Father broke into their kitchen as into a roomful of assassins, and confronted the glowering hulk of iron that was their stove. "Is it dirty or does it just look that way?"

She swallowed her temper, but with such bad grace there was no merit in it, only design. She gave the others such a terrible frown they all disappeared, even Sister Antonia.

Father squinted to read the name on the stove. "That stove cost a lot of money," he said. "They don't make them like that any more." He slapped the pipe going up and through the side of the wall. He gave the draft regulator a twist.

He went to the window and peered out. When he turned around he had the print of the screen on his nose. She would not say anything to distract him. He seemed to be thinking. Then he considered the stove again and appeared to have his mind made up. He faced her.

"The stove's all right, Sister. It won't draw properly, is all."

"I know, Father, but—"

"That tree," he said, pointing through the wall at the small tree which had been spared, "is blocking the draft. If you want your stove to work properly, it'll have to come down. That's all I got to say."

He squinted to read the name on the stove again.

She felt the blood assembling in patches on her cheeks. "Thank you, Father," she said, and went quickly out of the kitchen, only wanting to get upstairs and wash the money off her hands.

THE CORKERYS
by Frank O'Connor

May MacMahon was a good-looking girl, the only child of Jack MacMahon, the accountant, and his wife, Margaret. They lived in Cork, on Summerhill, the steep street that led from the flat of the city to the heights of Montenotte. She had always lived the life of a girl of good family, with piano lessons, dancing class, and crushes on her school friends' brothers. Only occasionally did she wonder what it was all about, and then she invariably forgot to ask her father, who would certainly know. Her father knew everything, or almost everything. He was a tall, shy, good-looking man who seemed to have been expecting martyrdom from his earliest years and drinking Irish whiskey to endure it. May's mother was small and pretty and very opinionated, though her opinions varied, and anyway did not last long. Her father's opinions never varied, and lasted forever.

When May became friendly with the Corkery family, it turned out that he had always had strong opinions about them as well. Mr. Corkery, a mild, inarticulate solicitor, whom May remembered going for lonely walks for the good of his health, had died and left his family with very limited means, but his widow had good connections and managed to provide an education (mostly free) for all six children. Of the boys, the eldest, Tim, was now a Dominican, and Joe, who came next in line, was also going in for the priesthood. The Church was in the family's blood, because Mrs. Corkery's brother was the Dean and her sister was Mother Superior of the convent of an enclosed order outside the city. Mrs. Corkery's nickname among the chil-

65

dren was "Reverend Mother," and they accused her of imitating her sister, but Mrs. Corkery only sniffed and said if everybody became priests and nuns there would be no Church left. Mrs. Corkery seemed to believe quite seriously that the needs of the Church were the only possible excuse for sex.

From knowing the Corkerys May began to realize at last what life was about. It was no longer necessary to ask her father. Anyway he wouldn't know. He and her mother were nice but commonplace. Everything they said and did was dull and predictable, and even when they went to Mass on Sunday they did so only because everyone else did it. The Corkerys were rarely dull and never predictable. Though their whole life seemed to center on the Church, they were not in the least pietistic. The Dean fought with Mrs. Corkery; Father Tim fought with Joe; the sisters fought with their brothers, who, they said, were getting all the attention, and fought one another when their brothers were not available. Tessie, the eldest girl, known as "The Limb of the Devil," or just "The Limb," was keeping company with a young stockbroker who told her a lot of dirty stories, which she repeated with great gusto to her brothers, particularly to Father Tim. This, however, was for family reasons, because they all agreed that Tim was inclined to put on airs.

And them The Limb astonished everybody by entering the convent where her aunt was Mother Superior. May attended the reception in the little convent chapel, which struck her to the heart by its combination of poverty and gentility. She felt that the ceremony might have been tolerable in a great cathedral with a choir and thundering organ, but not in that converted drawing room, where the nuns knelt along the side walls and squeaked like mourners. The Limb was laid out on the altar and first covered with roses as though she were dead; then an old nun clipped her long black hair with a shears. It fell and lay at her head as though it too had died. May drew a quick breath and glanced at Joe, who was kneeling beside her. Though he had his hand over his face, she knew from the way his shoulders moved that he was crying. Then she cried, too.

For a full week the ceremony gave her the horrors every time she remembered it, and she felt she should have nothing more to do with such an extraordinary family. All the same, a week with her parents was enough to make her realize the attraction of the Corkerys even more than before.

"Did it scare you, May?" Rosie, the second girl, asked with a wicked grin. "Cripes, it put the fear of God into me. I'm not having any of that *de profundis* stuff; I'm joining a decent missionary order." This was the first May had heard of Rosie's vocation. Inside a year, she, too, was in a convent, but in Rome, and "having a gas time," as she casually reported home.

They really were an extraordinary family, and the Dean was as queer as any of them. The Sunday following the ceremony May was at dinner there, and he put his hand firmly on her shoulder as though he were about to yank off her dress, and gave her a crooked smile that would have convinced any reasonable observer that he was a sex maniac, and yet May knew that almost every waking moment his thoughts were concentrated on outwitting the Bishop, who seemed to be the greatest enemy of the Church since Nero. The Bishop was a Dominican, and the Dean felt that a monk's place was in the cloister.

"The man is a bully!" he said, with an astonishment and grief that would have moved any audience but his own family.

"Oh, now Mick!" said Mrs. Corkery placidly. She was accustomed to hearing the Bishop denounced.

"I'm sorry, Josephine," the Dean said with a formal regret that rang equally untrue. "The man is a bully. An infernal bully, what's more. I'm not criticizing you or the order, Tim," he said, looking at his nephew over his spectacles, "but monks simply have no place in ecclesiastical affairs. Let them stick to their prayers is what I say."

"And a queer way the world would be only for them," Joe said. Joe was going for the secular priesthood himself, but he didn't like to see his overwhelming uncle get away with too much.

"Their influence on Church history has been disastrous!" the Dean bellowed, reaching for his cigarette case. "Always, or almost always, disastrous. That man thinks he knows everything."

"Maybe he does," said Joe.

"Maybe," said the Dean, like an old bull who cannot ignore a dart from any quarter. "But as well as that, he interferes in everything, and always publicly, always with the greatest possible amount of scandal. 'I don't like the model of that church;' 'Take away that statue;' 'That painting is irreverent.' Begob, Joe, I don't think even you know as much as that. I declare to God, Josephine, I believe if anyone suggested it to him that man would start inspecting the cut of the schoolgirls' panties." And when everyone roared with laughter, the Dean raised his head sternly and said, "I mean it."

Peter, the youngest boy, never got involved in these

family arguments about the Bishop, the orders, or the future of the Church. He was the odd man out. He was apprenticed in his father's old firm and would grow up to be owner or partner. In every Irish family there is a boy like Peter whose task it is to take on the family responsibilities. It was merely an accident that he was the youngest. What counted was that he was his mother's favorite. Even before he had a mind to make up, he knew it was not for him to become too involved, because someone would have to look after his mother in her old age. He might marry, but it would have to be a wife who suited her. He was the ugliest of the children, though with a monkey ugliness that was almost as attractive as Father Tim's film-star looks and Joe's ascetic masculine fire. He was slow, watchful, and good-humored, with high cheekbones that grew tiny bushes of hair, and he had a lazy malice that could often be as effective as the uproarious indignation of his brothers and sisters.

May, who saw the part he had been cast for, wondered whether she couldn't woo Mrs. Corkery as well as another girl.

After Rosie there was Joe, who was ordained the following year, and then Sheela did what seemed—in that family, at least—the conventional thing and went into the same convent as Tessie.

It was an extraordinary family, and May was never quite able to understand the fascination it had for her. Partly, of course—and this she felt rather that understood—it was the attraction of the large family for the only child, the sheer relief of never having to wonder what you were going to play next. But beside this there was an attraction rather like that of a large theatrical family—the feeling that everything was related to a larger imaginative world. In a sense, the Corkerys always seemed to be playing.

She knew that her own being in love with Peter was part of her love affair with the family as a whole, the longing to be connected with them, and the teasing she got about Peter from his brothers and sisters suggested that they, too, recognized it and were willing to accept her as one of themselves. But she also saw that her chance of ever marrying Peter was extremely slight, because Peter was not attracted by her. When he could have been out walking with her he was out walking with his friend Mick MacDonald, and when the pair of them came in while she was in the house, Peter behaved to her as though she were nothing more than a welcome stranger. He was always polite, always deferential—unlike Tim and Joe, who treated her as though she were an extra sister, to be slapped on the bottom or pushed out of the way as the mood struck them.

May was a serious girl; she had read books on modern psychology, and she knew that the very quality that made Peter settle for a life in the world made him unsuitable as a husband. It was strange how right the books were about that. He was dominated by his mother, and he could flirt with her as he never flirted with May. Clearly, no other woman would ever entirely replace his mother in his heart. In fact (May was too serious a girl not to give things their proper names), Peter was the very type of the homosexual —the latent homosexual, as she learned to call it.

Other boys *wanted* to go out with her, and she resented Peter's unfailing courtesy, though in more philosophic spells she realized that he probably couldn't help it, and that when he showed his almost boyish hero worship of Mick MacDonald before her it was not his fault but Nature's. All the same, she thought it very uncalled-for on the part of Nature, because it left her no particular interest in a world in which the only eligible young man was a queer. After a year or two of this, her thoughts turned more and more to the quiet convent where the Corkery girls contentedly carried on their simple lives of meditation and prayer. Once or twice she dropped a dark hint that she was thinking of becoming a nun herself, but each time it led to a scene with her father.

"You're a fool, girl!" he said harshly, getting up to pour himself an extra drink. May knew he didn't altogether resent being provoked, because it made him feel entitled to drink more.

"Now, Jack, you must not say things like that," her mother said anxiously.

"Of course I have to say it. Look at her! And she doesn't even have a boy!"

"But if there isn't a boy who interests her!"

"There are plenty of boys who'd interest her if only she behaved like a natural girl," he said gloomily. "What do you think a boy wants to do with a girl? Say the Rosary? She hasn't behaved naturally ever since she got friendly with that family—what's their name?"

"Corkery," Mrs. MacMahon said, having failed to perceive that not remembering the Corkery name was the one way the poor man had of getting back at them.

"Whatever their name is, they've turned her into an idiot. That's no great surprise. They never had any brains to distribute, themselves."

"But still, Jack, you will admit they've got on very well."

"They've got on very well!" he echoed scornfully. "In the Church! Except that young fellow, the solicitor's clerk,

and I suppose he hadn't brains enough even for the
Church. They should have put him in the friars.''

"But after all, their uncle is the Dean.''

"Wonderful Dean, too,'' grumbled Jack MacMahon.
"He drove me out of twelve o'clock Mass, so as not to
listen to his drivel. He can hardly speak decent English, not
to mind preaching a sermon. 'A bunch of baloney!''' he
quoted angrily. "If we had a proper bishop, instead of the
one we have, he'd make that fellow speak correctly in the
pulpit at least.''

"But it's only so that his congregation will understand
him, Jack.''

"Oh, his congregation understands him only too well.
Himself and his tall hat and his puffed-up airs! Common,
that's what he is, and that's what all the family are, on
both sides. If your daughter wants to be a nun, you and the
Corkerys can arrange it between you. But not one penny of
my money goes into their pockets, believe me!''

May was sorry to upset him, but for herself she did not
mind his loathing of the whole Corkery family. She knew
that it was only because he was fond of her and dreaded
being left without her in his old age. He had spoiled her so
long as she was not of an age to answer him back, and she
guessed he was looking forward to spoiling his grandchil-
dren even worse because he would not live long enough to
hear them answer him back. But this, she realized, was
what the Corkerys had done for her—made all that side of
life seem unimportant.

She had a long talk with Mother Agatha, Mrs. Corkery's
sister, about her vocation, which confirmed her in her res-
olution. Mother Agatha was very unlike her sister, who
was loud-voiced and humorous. The Mother Superior was
pale, thin, cool, and with the slightest trace of an ironic wit

that might have passed unnoticed by a stupider girl. But May noticed it, and realized that she was being observed very closely indeed.

She and her mother did the shopping for the trousseau, but the bills and parcels were kept carefully out of her father's sight. Drunk or sober, he refused to discuss the matter at all. "It would only upset him just now, poor man," her mother said philosophically. He was drinking heavily, and when he was in liquor he quarrelled a lot with her mother about little things. With May he avoided quarrels, or even arguments, and it struck her that he was training himself for a life in which he would no longer have her to quarrel with. On the day of the reception he did not drink at all, which pleased her, and was icily polite to everybody, but when, later, she appeared behind the parlor grille, all in white, and the sun caught her, she saw his face in the darkness of the parlor, with all the life drained out of it, and suddenly he turned and left without a word. It was only then that a real feeling of guilt sprang up in her at the thought of the miserable old age that awaited him—a man like him, who loved young creatures who could not answer him back, and who would explain to them unweariedly about the sun and moon and geography and figures. She had answered him back in a way that left him with nothing to look forward to.

All the same, there was something very comforting about the life of an enclosed order. It had been organized a long, long time before, by people who knew more about the intrusions of the outside world than May did. The panics that had seized her about her ability to sustain her life diminished and finally ceased. The round of duties, services, and mortifications was exactly what she had

needed, and little by little she felt the last traces of
worldliness slip from her—even the very human worry
about the old age of her father and mother. The convent
was poor, and not altogether from choice. Everything in
the house was mean and clean and cheerful, and May grew
to love the old drawing room that had been turned into a
chapel, where she knelt, in her own place, through the
black winter mornings when at home she would still be
tucked up comfortably in bed. She liked the rough feeling
of her clothes and the cold of the floor through her sandals, though mostly she liked the proximity of Tessie and
Sheela.

There were times when, reading the lives of the saints,
she wished she had lived in more heroic times, and she secretly invented minor mortifications for herself to make
sure she could endure them. It was not until she had been
in the convent for close on a year that she noticed that the
minor mortifications were liable to be followed by major
depressions. Though she was a clever woman, she did not
try to analyze this. She merely lay awake at night and realized that the nuns she lived with—given Tessie and Sheela
—were not the stuff of saints and martyrs but ordinary
women who behaved in religion very much as they would
have behaved in marriage, and who followed the rule in the
spirit in which her father went to Mass on Sundays. There
was nothing whatever to be said against them, and any
man who had got one of them for a wife would probably
have considered himself fortunate, but all the same, there
was something about them that was not quite grown-up. It
was very peculiar and caused her great concern. The things
that had really frightened her about the order when she
was in the world—the loneliness, the austerity, the ruthless
discipline—now seemed to her meaningless and harmless.

After that she saw with horror that the great days of the Church were over, and that they were merely a lot of perfectly commonplace women play-acting austerity and meditation.

"But my dear child," Mother Agatha said when May wept out her story to her, "of course we're only children. Of course we're only play-acting. How else does a child learn obedience and discipline?"

And when May talked to her about what the order had been in earlier days, that vague, ironic note crept into Mother Superior's voice, as though she had heard it all many times before. "I know, Sister," she said, with a nod. "Believe me, I do know that the order was stricter in earlier times. But you must remember that it was not founded in a semi-arctic climate like ours, so there was less chance of the sisters' dying of double pneumonia. I have talked to half the plumbers in town, but it seems that central heating is not understood here. . . . Everything is relative. I'm sure we suffer just as much in our very comfortable sandals as the early sisters suffered in their bare feet, and probably at times rather more, but at any rate we are not here for the sole purpose of suffering mortification, whatever pleasures it may hold for us."

Every word Mother Agatha said made perfect sense to May while she was saying it, and May knew she was being ungrateful and hysterical, but when the interview was over and the sound of her sobs had died away, she was left with the impression that Mother Agatha was only another commonplace woman, with a cool manner and a sarcastic tongue, who was also acting the part of a nun. She was alone in a world of bad actors and actresses, and the Catholicism she had known and believed in was dead.

A few weeks later she was taken to a private nursing

home. "Just for a short rest, Sister," as Mother Agatha said. "It's a very pleasant place, and you will find a lot of other religious there who need a rest as well."

There followed an endless but timeless phase of weeping and confusion, when all May's ordinary life was broken up and strange men burst into her room and examined her and asked questions she did not understand and replied to questions of hers in a way that showed they had not understood them either. Nobody seemed to realize that she was the last Catholic in the world; nobody understood her tears about it. Above all, nobody seemed to be able to hear the gramophone record that played continuously in her head, and that stopped only when they gave her an injection.

Then, one Spring day, she went into the garden for a walk and a young nurse saw her back to her room. Far ahead of them, at the other end of a long, white corridor, she saw an old man with his back to her, and remembered that she had seen his face many times before and had perceived, without paying attention to, his long, gloomy, ironic face. She knew she must have remembered him, because now she could see nothing but his back, and suddenly the words "Who is that queer old man?" broke through the sound of the gramophone record, surprising her as much as they seemed to surprise the young nurse.

"Oh, him!" the nurse said, with a smile. "Don't you know him? He's here for years."

"But why, Nurse?"

"Oh, he doesn't think he's a priest, and he is one really, that's the trouble."

"But how extraordinary!"

"Isn't it?" the nurse said, biting her lower lip in a smile. "Cripes, you'd think 'twas something you wouldn't forget. He's nice, really, though," she added gravely, as though she felt she had been criticizing him.

When they reached May's room, the young nurse grinned again, in a guilty way, and May noticed that she was extravagantly pretty, with small, gleaming front teeth.

"*You're* getting all right, anyway," she said.

"Oh, really?" May said vaguely, because she knew she was getting all right. "Why do you think that, Nurse?"

"Oh, you get to spot things," the nurse said with a shrug, and left May uncomforted, because she didn't know if she really did get well how she could face the convent and the other nuns again. All of them, she felt, would be laughing at her. Instead of worrying about the nuns, she went into a mournful daydream about the old priest who did not think he was a priest, and next day, when her father called, she said intensely, "Daddy, there's a priest in here who doesn't believe he's a priest—isn't that extraordinary?" She did not hear the tone of her own voice or know how reasonable it sounded, and so she was surprised when her father looked away and started fumbling mechanically in his jacket pocket for a cigarette.

"Well, you don't have to think you're a nun either," he said, with an unsteady voice. "Your mother has your own room ready for you when you come home."

"Oh, but Daddy, I have to go back to the convent."

"Oh, no you don't. No more convents for you, young lady! That's fixed up already with Mother Superior. It was all a mistake from the beginning. You're coming straight home to your mother and me."

Then May knew she was really going to get well, and she wanted to go home with him at once, not to go back up the stairs behind the big iron door where there was always an attendant on duty. She knew that going back home meant defeat, humiliation, and despair, but she no longer cared even about that. She just wanted to take up her life again at the point where it had gone wrong, when she had first met the Corkerys.

Her father brought her home and acted as though he had rescued her from a dragon's den. Each evening, when he came home from work, he sat with her, sipping at his drink and talking quietly and comfortably. She felt he was making great efforts to assure that she felt protected and relaxed. Most of the time she did, but there were spells when she wanted her mother to put her back in the nursing home.

"Oh, I couldn't do that," her mother said characteristically. "It would upset your poor father too much."

But she did discuss it with the doctor—a young man, thin and rather unhealthy-looking, who looked as though he, too, was living on his nerves—and he argued with May about it.

"But what am I to do, Doctor, when I feel like this?" she asked plaintively.

"Go out and get jarred," he said briskly.

"Get what, Doctor?" she asked feebly.

"Jarred," he repeated without embarrassment. "Stoned. Polluted. Drunk. I don't mean alone, of course. You need a young fellow along with you."

"Oh, not that again, Doctor!" she said, and for some reason her voice came out exactly like Mother Agatha's—which was not how she intended it to sound.

"And some sort of a job," he went on remorselessly. "There isn't a damn thing wrong with you except that you think you're a failure. You're not, of course, but as a result of thinking you are you've scratched the surface of your mind all over, and when you sit here like this, looking out at the rain, you keep rubbing it so that it doesn't heal. Booze, lovemaking, and hard work—they keep your hands away from the sore surface, and then it heals of its own accord.''

She did her best, but it didn't seem to heal as easily as all that. Her father got her a job in the office of a friend, and she listened, in fascination, to the chatter of the other secretaries. She even went out in the evening with a couple of them and listened to their common little love stories. She knew if she had to wait until she talked like that about fellows in order to be well, her case was hopeless. Instead, she got drunk and told them how she had been for years in love with a homosexual, and, as she told it, the story became so hopeless and dreadful that she sobbed over it herself. After that she went home and wept for hours, because she knew that she had been telling lies, and betrayed the only people in the world whom she had really cared for.

Her father made a point of never referring at all to the Corkerys, the convent, or the nursing home. She knew that for him this represented a real triumph of character, because he loathed the Corkerys more than ever for what he believed they had done to her. But even he could not very well ignore the latest development in the saga. It seemed that Mrs. Corkery herself had decided to become a nun. She announced placidly to everyone that she had done her duty by her family, who were now all comfortably settled, and that she felt free to do what she had always wanted to do anyhow. She discussed it with the Dean, who practically excommunicated her on the spot. He said the family would never live down the scandal, and Mrs. Corkery told him it wasn't the scandal that worried him at all but the loss of the one house where he could get a decent meal. If he had a spark of manliness, she said, he would get rid of his housekeeper, who couldn't cook, was a miserable sloven, and ordered him about as if he were a schoolboy. The Dean said she would have to get permission in writing from every one of her children, and Mrs. Corkery replied calmly that there was no difficulty whatever about that.

May's father didn't really want to crow, but he could not resist pointing out that he had always said the Corkerys had a slate loose.

"I don't see anything very queer about it," May said stubbornly.

"A woman with six children entering a convent at her age!" her father said, not even troubling to grow angry with her. "Even the Dean realizes it's mad."

"It *is* a little bit extreme, all right," her mother said, with a frown, but May knew she was thinking of her.

May had the feeling that Mrs. Corkery would make a very good nun if for no other reason than to put her brother and Mother Agatha in their place. And of course, there were other reasons. As a girl she had wanted to be a nun, but for family reasons it was impossible, so she had become a good wife and mother, instead. Now, after thirty years of pinching and scraping, her family had grown away from her and she could return to her early dream. There was nothing unbalanced about that, May thought bitterly. *She* was the one who had proven unbalanced.

For a while it plunged her back into gloomy moods, and they were made worse by the scraps of gossip that people passed on to her, not knowing how they hurt. Mrs. Corkery had collected her six letters of freedom and taken them herself to the Bishop, who had immediately given in. "Spite!" the Dean pronounced gloomily. "Nothing but spite—all because I don't support his mad dream of turning a modern city into a medieval monastery."

On the day of Mrs. Corkery's reception, May did not leave the house at all. It rained, and she sat by the sitting-room window, looking across the city to where the hills were almost invisible. She was living Mrs. Corkery's day through—the last day in the human world of an old woman who had assumed the burden she herself had been too weak to accept. She could see it all as though she were back in that mean, bright little chapel, with the old woman lying out on the altar, covered with roses like a corpse, and an old nun shearing off her thin gray locks. It was all so intolerably vivid that May kept bursting into sudden fits of tears and whimpering like a child.

One evening a few weeks later, she came out of the office in the rain and saw Peter Corkery at the other side of the street. She obeyed her first instinct and bowed her head so as not to look at him. Her heart sank as he crossed the road to accost her.

"Aren't you a great stranger, May?" he asked, with his cheerful grin.

"We're very busy in the office these days, Peter," she replied, with false brightness.

"It was only the other night Joe was talking about you. You know Joe is up in the seminary now?"

"No. What's he doing?"

"Teaching. He finds it a great relief after the mountains. And, of course, you know about the mother." This was it!

"I heard about it. I suppose ye're all delighted?"

"*I* wasn't very delighted," he said, and his lips twisted in pain. "'Twas the most awful day I ever spent. When they cut off her hair—"

"You don't have to remind me."

"I disgraced myself, May. I had to run out of the chapel. And here I had two nuns after me, trying to steer

me to the lavatory. Why do nuns always think a man is
looking for a lavatory?"

"I wouldn't know. I wasn't a very good one."

"There are different opinions about that," he said
gently, but he only hurt her more.

"And I suppose you'll be next?"

"How next?"

"I was sure you had a vocation, too."

"I don't know," he said thoughtfully. "I never really
asked myself. I suppose, in a way, it depends on you."

"And what have I to say to it?" she asked in a ladylike
tone, though her heart suddenly began to pant.

"Only whether you're going to marry me or not. Now I
have the house to myself and only Mrs. Maher looking
after me. You remember Mrs. Maher?"

"And you think I'd made a cheap substitute for Mrs.
Maher, I suppose?" she asked, and suddenly all the pent-
up anger and frustration of years seemed to explode inside
her. She realized that it was entirely because of him that
she had become a nun, because of him she had been locked
up in a nursing home and lived the live of an emotional
cripple. "Don't you think that's an extraordinary sort of
proposal—if it's intended to be a proposal."

"Why the hell should I be any good at proposing? How
many girls do you think I've proposed to?"

"Not many, since they didn't teach you better manners.
And it would never occur to yourself to say you loved me.
Do you?" she almost shouted. "Do you love me?"

"Sure, of course I do," he said, almost in astonishment.
"I wouldn't be asking you to marry me otherwise. But all
the same—"

"All the same, all the same, you have reservations!"
And suddenly language that would have appalled her to

hear a few months before broke from her, before she burst into uncontrollable tears and went running homeward through the rain. "God damn you to Hell, Peter Corkery! I wasted my life on you, and now in the heel of the hunt all you can say to me is 'All the same.' You'd better go back to your damn pansy pals, and say it to them."

She was hysterical by the time she reached Summerhill. Her father's behavior was completely characteristic. He was a born martyr and this was only another of the ordeals for which he had been preparing himself all his life. He got up and poured himself a drink.

"Well, there is one thing I'd better tell you now, daughter," he said quietly but firmly. "That man will never enter this house in my lifetime."

"Oh, nonsense, Jack MacMahon!" his wife said in a rage, and she went and poured herself a drink, a thing she did under her husband's eye only when she was preparing to fling it at him. "You haven't a scrap of sense. Don't you see now that the boy's mother only entered the convent because she knew he'd never feel free while she was in the world?"

"Oh, Mother!" May cried, startled out of her hysterics.

"Well, am I right?" her mother said, drawing herself up.

"Oh, you're right, you're right." May said, beginning to sob again. "Only I was such a fool it never occurred to me. Of course, she was doing it for me."

"And for her son," said her mother. "And if he's anything like his mother, I'll be very proud to claim him for a son-in-law."

She looked at her husband, but saw that she had made her effect and could now enjoy her drink in peace. "Of course, in some ways it's going to be very embarrassing," she went on peaceably. "We can't very well say 'Mr. Peter Corkery, son of Sister Rosina of the Little Flower' or whatever the dear lady's name is. In fact, it's very difficult to see how we're going to get it into the press at all. However, as I always say, if the worst comes to the worst, there's a lot to be said for a quiet wedding. . . . I do hope you were nice to him, May?" she asked.

It was only then that May remembered that she hadn't been in the least nice and, in fact, had used language that would have horrified her mother. Not that it would make much difference. She and Peter had travelled so far together, and by such extraordinary ways.

MINUTES OF THE MEETING
by Sister Rose Tillemans

The regular monthly house meeting of the Sisters of Our Lady of Perpetual Succor Convent was held in the community room November 20, 1976 at 5:00 P.M. Everyone was present except Sister Joleen who was calling Bingo at the Parish Center. Sister Placidia, our coordinatory, chaired the meeting. Sister opened with prayer, asking help for each of us in controlling our feelings and entering into the discussions with a spirit of charity, respecting the opinions of others and not saying anything which we would later regret. The minutes of the last meeting were read and approved. Sister Placidia said the meeting would terminate in an hour and any left over business would be tabled until next time.

The first item on the agenda, Sister Placidia stated, was a request she had received from Monsignor O'Driscoll that all the sisters of Our Lady of Perpetual Succor School wear veils. The sisters of OLPSS, he said, had been in veils since the opening of the school in 1926 until this fall when the two new sisters came. He wanted all the sisters to stand veiled as a bulwark upholding the traditions of the Church. Sister Placidia felt we should all comply with Monsignor because he had never made many demands on us, was an old man, had a weak heart and just yesterday had sent us a lovely 25-pound Thanksgiving turkey. Sister Bev said that in no way was any man going to tell her what to wear, particularly O'Driscoll, who had not set foot in school this year. Sister Lou told Sister Placidia that if O'Driscoll wanted a nun with a veil in her classroom he would have to look elsewhere for a third grade teacher. Sister John Paul commented that her veil told a perverted and pornographic world that she was chaste. Sister Phillip said that although she was 75 she had for a long time entertained a yen to drop the veil but had not done so because of her bald spot and deference to Monsignor. Sister Enda announced that she was glad she had a veil to separate her from the seculars. Sister Lou said that she didn't think being a secular was so low-brow. Jesus had chosen to be a secular and proclaimed his message without aid of outward sign, i.e., habit, Roman collar or veil. Sister Reynolds voiced her opinion that the classroom staffed by sisters with veils had better discipline. Both Sisters Bev and Lou challenged her statement, and several other sisters challenged Sisters Bev and Lou. Sister Mary Louise asked to be excused to take a Darvon, and Sister Emerance opened the north windows. Sister Placidia reminded us of the opening prayer.

Sister Cuthberta said if we were finished with the veils she'd like to say that there had been an awful lot of drips in the dining room lately and would we be more careful.

Sister Enda asked that if we had to bring seculars around the house would we keep them out of the bedroom area.

Sister Lou stated that she thought we should ask the parish for another car. She did not feel that two cars were enough for thirty people. It was Sister Josithea's opinion that three cars parked in front of the convent would be against poverty. Sister Bev said there were three priests in the rectory and three cars parked out in front, and that the ratio at the convent was unbalanced. Sister Josithea argued that the priests did not have a vow of poverty. Sister Lynette told us that we couldn't keep two sign-out car-books straight now and how could we manage a third. Also, she said, since she was in charge of car maintenance would the person who dented the rear end of the Malibu report to her after the meeting. Sister Bev said that whenever she tried to sign out a car for a meeting or a visit to shut-ins it was reserved for a wake or funeral. We should, added Sister Bev, be where the pulse is if we are to witness to the world. Sister Raynolds felt that we should also be where the pulse is not because the Church had always exhorted us to pray for the dead. A discussion followed as to which was most important relating our use of the cars, the living or the dead. No decision was reached, but Sister Lou felt that a third car would take care of both needs.

Sister Placidia asked us to recall the opening prayer, and Sister Emerance opened the west windows.

Sister Cuthberta said Warren would be around Monday to fix the leaking radiators. We should put a note on the board telling where the leaks are.

Sister Gratia asked if it would be all right to bring her eighth grade girls to the convent for a prayer day Friday. She felt that if the girls saw what the inside of a real convent was like they might want to be sisters. Sister Cuthberta said that Warren had just waxed all the floors and it would be a shame to track them up. Sister Enda objected because she felt the convent was the sisters' private home and should not be over-run by a bunch of teenagers. Sister Gratia said she understood and knew that her sister and brother-in-law would let her use their home for the prayer day. Sister Placidia commended Sister Gratia for her gentle acceptance of the sisters' wishes and told her that she reminded her a lot of the Little Flower.

Sister Mary Louise suggested that we try to keep a more even beat in reciting the office. The Blessed Virgin's side was dragging terribly, she said. Sister Jacqueline expressed the opinion that if there was one place we shouldn't have to speed, it was at prayer. Sister Alice Bernard said she liked it on St. Joseph's side and wished more people would sit there. She said the pace was livelier.

Sister Elvira reported that there were a lot of extra *Wanderers* for the taking in the back of the church.

Sister Bev felt we should do something about forming community in the house. There was no coming together, she said, no indepth relationships or real sharing of our lives, and very little communication. She said she often felt lonely even with thirty people. Sister Ulrica said she had experienced a real togetherness the other night at TV when at least eight people were watching "All in the Family" enjoying Archie, Edith and Meathead. She suggested that Sister Bev come to TV more. Sister Enda told us that after being with seculars all day she wanted to be alone at night. Sister Mirabilia said that she understood what Sister Bev meant and that maybe what we needed was healing. Her charismatic group was sponsoring a healing workshop at St. Odelia's next weekend and that maybe we should all sign up, at least those with deep wounds. Sister Placidia didn't think we needed to do anything that drastic and suggested that each sister spend a little extra time in the chapel every day praying for the needs of the house. She would ask Monsignor to say a mass for a special intention. Sister Bev said that we shouldn't ask God to perform miracles for us if we weren't ready to do something about ourselves at the gut level. Sister Clementia expressed the view that the level Sister Bev was referring to was not a part of her vocabulary and would she call it something else. Sister Delvita thought that planning a Christmas party might help form community. Working on committees would provide us with opportunities to get acquainted. Sister Placidia appointed Sisters Bev and Gratia to co-chair the Christmas party. It would be nice to invite Monsignor and the two assistants, she said.

Sister Jane Ann asked that we notify her at least four days in advance if we were going to have a guest for dinner. We are to indicate on the guest calendar the nature of the person invited, i.e., P for priest, S for sister and Se for secular. It makes a difference in planning the menu, she said.

Sister Enda requested that we tell our friends and relatives not to call the convent after 9:00 because the sisters needed their rest when they had worked hard all day. Sister said she sleeps next to the telephone and minds being roused at all hours.

Sister Cuthberta reported that Warren had told her too many people were tampering with the thermostat and that only she and he were to touch it. Warren said the thermostat was like a delicate person and had to be treated with care. Sister Placidia told Sister Cuthberta that she appreciated the way she and Warren were trying to control the heat and did everyone understand who were the two people who were to regulate the thermostat.

We were asked by Sister Placidia to sign the thank you card on the table to Monsignor for the lovely 25-pound Thanksgiving turkey.

Sisters Bev and Lou announced their intention to move into an apartment and work in the inner city next year.

Sister Placidia asked if there were any further business.

Sister LuAnne indicated that the hour was up and it was time for Lawrence Welk. Sister Placidia said that since Lawrence Welk was coming on directly she would dispense with the closing prayer. The meeting was adjourned. Sister Emerance closed the north and west windows.

Respectfully submitted.
Sister Eldora Krunkel

IN THE REGION OF ICE
by Joyce Carol Oates

Sister Irene was a tall, deft woman in her early thirties. What one could see of her face made a striking impression—serious hard gray eyes, a long slender nose, a face waxen with thought. Seen at the right time, from the right angle, she was almost handsome; in her past teaching positions she had drawn a little upon the fact of her being young and brilliant and also a nun, but she was beginning to grow out of that.

This was a new university and an entirely new world. She had heard—of course it was true—that the Jesuit administration of this school had hired her at the last moment to save money and to head off the appointment of a man of dubious religious commitment. She had prayed for the necessary energy to get her through this first semester. She had no trouble with teaching itself; once she stood before a classroom she felt herself capable of anything. It was the world immediately outside the classroom that confused and alarmed her, though she let none of this show—the cynicism of her colleagues, the indifference of many of the students, and above all, the looks she got that told her nothing much would be expected of her because she was a nun. This took energy, strength. At times she had the idea that she was on trial and that the excuses she made to herself about her discomfort were only the common excuses made by guilty people. But in front of a class she had no time to worry about herself or the conflicts in her mind. She became, once and for all, a figure existing only for the benefit of others, an instrument by which facts were communicated.

About two weeks after the semester began, Sister Irene noticed a new student in her class. He was slight and fair-haired, and his face was blank, but not blank by accident, blank on purpose, suppressed and restricted into a dumbness that looked hysterical. She was prepared for him before he raised his hand, and when she saw his arm jerk, as if he had at last lost control of it, she nodded to him without hesitation.

"Sister, how can this be reconciled with Shakespeare's vision in *Hamlet?* How can these opposing views be in the same mind?"

Students glanced at him, mildly surprised. He did not belong in the class, and this was mysterious, but his manner was urgent and blind.

"There is no need to reconcile opposing views," Sister Irene said, leaning forward against the podium. "In one play Shakespeare suggests one vision, in another play another; the plays are not simultaneous creations, and even if they were, we never demand a logical—"

"We must demand a logical consistency," the young man said. "The idea of education itself is predicated upon consistency, order, sanity—"

He had interrupted her, and she hardened her face against him—for his sake, not her own, since she did not really care. But he noticed nothing. "Please see me after class," she said.

After class the young man hurried up to her.

"Sister Irene, I hope you didn't mind my visiting today. I'd heard some things, interesting things," he said. He stared at her, and something in her face allowed him to smile. "I—could we talk in your office? Do you have time?"

They walked down to her office. Sister Irene sat at her

desk, and the young man sat facing her; for a moment they were self-conscious and silent.

"Well, I suppose you know—I'm a Jew," he said.

Sister Irene stared at him. "Yes?" she said.

"What am I doing at a Catholic university, huh?" He grinned. "That's what you want to know."

She made a vague movement of her hand to show that she had no thoughts on this, nothing at all, but he seemed not to catch it. He was sitting on the edge of the straight-backed chair. She saw that he was young but did not really look young. There were harsh lines on either side of his mouth, as if he had misused that youthful mouth some-how. His skin was almost as pale as hers, his eyes were dark and somehow not quite in focus. He looked at her and through her and around her, as his voice surrounded them both. His voice was a little shrill at times.

"Listen, I did the right thing today—visiting your class! God, what a lucky accident it was; some jerk mentioned you, said you were a good teacher—I thought, what a laugh! These people know about good teachers, here? But yes, listen, yes, I'm not kidding—you are good. I mean that."

Sister Irene frowned. "I don't quite understand what all this means."

He smiled and waved aside her formality, as if he knew better. "Listen, I got my B.A. at Columbia, then I came back here to his crappy city. I mean, I did it on purpose, I wanted to come back. I wanted to. I have my reasons for doing things. I'm on a three-thousand-dollar fellowship," he said, and waited for that to impress her. "You know, I could have gone almost anywhere with that fellowship, and I came back home here—my home's in the city—and enrolled here. This was last year. This is my second year.

I'm working on a thesis, I mean I was, my master's thesis
—but the hell with that. What I want to ask you is this:
Can I enroll in your class, is it too late? We have to get special permission if we're late.''

Sister Irene felt something nudging her, some uneasiness
in him that was pleading with her not to be offended by his
abrupt, familiar manner. He seemed to be promising another self, a better self, as if his fair, childish, almost
cherubic face was doing tricks to distract her from what his
words said.

"Are you in English studies?'' she asked.

"I was in history. Listen,'' he said, and his mouth did
something odd, drawing itself down into a smile that made
the lines about it deepen like knives, "listen, they kicked
me out.''

He sat back, watching her. He crossed his legs. He took
out a package of cigarettes and offered her one. Sister
shook her head, staring at his hands. They were small and
stubby and might have belonged to a ten-year-old, and the
nails were a strange near-violet color. It took him a while
to extract a cigarette.

"Yeah, kicked me out. What do you think of that?''

"I don't understand.''

"My master's thesis was coming along beautifully, and
then this bastard—I mean, excuse me, this professor, I
won't pollute your office with his name—he started making criticisms, he said some things were unacceptable,
he—'' The boy leaned forward and hunched his narrow
shoulders in a parody of secrecy. "We had an argument. I
told him some frank things, things only a broadminded
person could hear about himself. That takes courage,
right? He didn't have it! He kicked me out of the master's
program, so now I'm coming into English. Literature is

greater than history; European history is one big pile of
garbage. Skyhigh. Filth and rotting corpses, right? Aris-
totle says that poetry is higher than history; he's right; in
your class today I suddenly realized that this is my field,
Shakespeare, only Shakespeare is—"

Sister Irene guessed that he was going to say that only
Shakespeare was equal to him, and she caught the moment
of recognition and hesitation, the half-raised arm, the
keen, frowning forehead, the narrowed eyes; then he
thought better of it and did not end the sentence. "The students in your class are mainly neglible, I can tell you that.
You're new here, and I've been here a year—I would have
finished my studies last year but my father got sick, he was
hospitalized, I couldn't take exams and it was a mess—but
I'll make it through English in one year or drop dead. I can
do it, I can do anything. I'll take six courses at once—" He
broke off, breathless. Sister Irene tried to smile. "All
right, then, it's settled? You'll let me in? Have I missed
anything so far?"

He had no idea of the rudeness of his question. Sister
Irene, feeling suddenly exhausted, said, "I'll give you a syl-
labus of the course."

"Fine! Wonderful!"

He got to his feet eagerly. He looked through the schedule, muttering to himself, making favorable noises. It
struck Sister Irene that she was making a mistake to let him
in. There were these moments when one had to make an intelligent decision. . . . But she was sympathetic with him,
yes. She was sympathetic with something about him.

She found out his name the next day: Allen Weinstein.

After this, she came to her Shakespeare class with a
sense of excitement. It became clear to her at once that
Weinstein was the most intelligent student in the class. Un-

til he had enrolled, she had not understood what was lacking, a mind that could appreciate her own. Within a week his jagged, protean mind had alienated the other students, and though he sat in the center of the class, he seemed totally alone, encased by a miniature world of his own. When he spoke of the "frenetic humanism of the High Renaissance," Sister Irene dreaded the raised eyebrows and mocking smiles of the other students, who no longer bothered to look at Weinstein. She wanted to defend him, but she never did, because there was something rude and dismal about his knowledge; he used it like a weapon, talking passionately of Nietzsche and Goethe and Freud until Sister Irene would be forced to close discussion.

In meditation, alone, she often thought of him. When she tried to talk about him to a young nun, Sister Carlotta, everything sounded gross. "But no, he's an excellent student," she insisted. "I'm very grateful to have him in class. It's just that . . . he thinks ideas are real." Sister Carlotta, who loved literature also, had been forced to teach grade-school arithmetic for the last four years. That might have been why she said, a little sharply, "You don't think ideas are real?"

Sister Irene acquiesced with a smile, but of course she did not think so: only reality is real.

When Weinstein did not show up for class on the day the first paper was due, Sister Irene's heart sank, and the sensation was somehow a familiar one. She began her lecture and kept waiting for the door to open and for him to hurry noisily back to his seat, grinning an apology toward her—but nothing happened.

If she had been deceived by him, she made herself think angrily, it was as a teacher and not as a woman. He had promised her nothing.

Weinstein appeared the next day near the steps of the

liberal arts building. She heard someone running behind her, a breathless exclamation: "Sister Irene!" She turned and saw him, panting and grinning in embarrassment. He wore a dark-blue suit with a necktie, and he looked, despite his childish face, like a little old man; there was something oddly precarious and fragile about him. "Sister Irene, I owe you an apology, right?" He raised his eyebrows and smiled a sad, forlorn, yet irritatingly conspiratorial smile. "The first paper—not in on time, and I know what your rules are. . . . You won't accept late papers, I know—that's good discipline, I'll do that when I teach, too. But, unavoidably, I was unable to come to school yesterday. There are many—many—" He gulped for breath, and Sister Irene had the startling sense of seeing the real Weinstein stare out at her, a terrified prisoner behind the confident voice. "There are many complications in family life. Perhaps you are unaware—I mean—"

She did not like him, but she felt this sympathy, something tugging and nagging at her the way her parents had competed for her love, so many years ago. They had been whining, weak people, and out of their wet need for affection, the girl she had been (her name was Yvonne) had emerged stronger than either of them, contemptuous of tears because she had seen so many. But Weinstein was different; he was not simply weak, perhaps he was not weak at all, but his strength was confused and hysterical. She felt her customary rigidity as a teacher begin to falter. "You may turn your paper in today, if you have it," she said, frowning.

Weinstein's mouth jerked into an incredulous grin. "Wonderful! Marvelous!" he said. "You are very understanding, Sister Irene, I must say. I must say . . . I didn't expect, really. . . ." He was fumbling in a shabby old brief-case for the paper. Sister Irene waited. She was prepared for another of his excuses, certain that he did not have the paper, when he suddenly straightened up and handed her something. "Here! I took the liberty of writing thirty pages instead of just fifteen," he said. He was obviously quite excited; his cheeks were mottled pink and white. "You may disagree violently with my interpretation—I ex-pect you to, in fact I'm counting on it—but let me warn you, I have the exact proof, precise, specific proof, right here in the play itself!" He was thumping at a book, his voice growing louder and shriller. Sister Irene, startled, wanted to put her hand over his mouth and soothe him.

"Look," he said breathlessly, "may I talk with you? I have a class now I hate, I loathe, I can't bear to sit through! Can I talk with you instead?"

Because she was nervous, she stared at the title page of the paper: "Erotic Melodies in *Romeo and Juliet*" by Allen Weinstein, Jr.

"All right?" he said. "Can we walk around here? Is it all right? I've been anxious to talk with you about some things you said in class."

She was reluctant, but he seemed not to notice. They walked slowly along the shaded campus paths. Weinstein did all the talking, of course, and Sister Irene recognized nothing in his cascade of words that she had mentioned in class. "The humanist must be committed to the totality of life," he said passionately. "This is the failing one finds everywhere in the academic world! I found it in New York and I found it here and I'm no ingénue, I don't go around with my mouth hanging open—I'm experienced, look, I've been to Europe, I've lived in Rome! I went everywhere in

Europe except Germany, I don't talk about Germany. . . .
Sister Irene, think of the significant men in the last century, the men who've changed the world! Jews, right?
Marx, Freud, Einstein! Not that I believe Marx, Marx is a
madman . . . and Freud, no, my sympathies are with spiritual humanism. I believe that the Jewish race is the exclusive . . . the exclusive, what's the word, the exclusive means
by which humanism will be extended. . . . Humanism be-
gins by excluding the Jew, and now," he said, with a high,
surprised laugh, "the Jew will perfect it. After the Nazis,
only the Jew is authorized to understand humanism, its
limitations and its possibilities. So, I say that the humanist
is committed to life in its totality and not just to his profession! The religious person is totally religious, he *is* his religion! What else? I recognize in you a humanist and a religious person—"

But he did not seem to be talking to her, or even looking
at her. "Here, read this," he said. "I wrote it last night."
It was a long free-verse poem, typed on a typewriter
whose ribbon was worn out. "There's this trouble with my
father, a wonderful man, a lovely man, but his health—his
strength is fading, do you see? What must it be to him to
see his son growing up? I mean, I'm a man now, he's getting old, weak, his health is bad—it's hell, right? I sym-
pathize with him. I'd do anything for him, I'd cut open my
veins, anything for a father—right? That's why I wasn't in
school yesterday," he said, and his voice dropped for the
last sentence, as if he had been dragged back to earth by a
fact.

Sister Irene tried to read the poem, then pretended to
read it. A jumble of words dealing with "life" and
"death" and "darkness" and "love." "What do you

think?'' Weinstein said nervously, trying to read it over her shoulder and crowding against her.

"It's very . . . passionate," Sister Irene said.

This was the right comment; he took the poem back from her in silence, his face flushed with excitement. "Here, at this school, I have few people to talk with. I haven't shown anyone else that poem." He looked at her with his dark, intense eyes, and Sister Irene felt them focus upon her. She was terrified at what he was trying to do—he was trying to force her into a human relationship.

"Thank you for your paper," she said, turning away.

When he came the next day, ten minutes late, he was haughty and disdainful. He had nothing to say and sat with his arms folded. Sister Irene took back with her to the convent a feeling of betrayal and confusion. She had been hurt. It was absurd, and yet— She spent too much time thinking about him, as if he were somehow a kind of crystallization of her own loneliness; but she had no right to think so much of him. She did not want to think of him or of her loneliness. But Weinstein did so much more than think of his predicament, he embodied it, he acted it out, and that was perhaps why he fascinated her. It was as if he were doing a dance for her, a dance of shame and agony and delight, and so long as he did it, she was safe. She felt embarrassment for him, but also anxiety; she wanted to protect him. When the dean of the graduate school questioned her about Weinstein's work, she insisted that he was an "excellent" student, though she knew the dean had not wanted to hear that.

She prayed for guidance, she spent hours on her devotions, she was closer to her vocation than she had been for some years. Life at the convent became tinged with unreality, a misty distortion that took its tone from the glowering skies of the city at night, identical smokestacks ranged against the clouds and giving to the sky the excrement of the populated and successful earth. This city was not her city, this world was not her world. She felt no pride in knowing this, it was a fact. The little convent was not like an island in the center of this noisy world, but rather a kind of hole or crevice the world did not bother with, something of no interest. The convent's rhythm of life had nothing to do with the world's rhythm, it did not violate or alarm it in any way. Sister Irene tried to draw together the fragments of her life and synthesize them somehow in her vocation as a nun: she was a nun, she was recognized as a nun and had given herself happily to that life, she had a name, a place, she had dedicated her superior intelligence to the Church, she worked without pay and without expecting gratitude, she had given up pride, she did not think of herself but only of her work and her vocation, she did not think of anything external to these, she saturated herself daily in the knowledge that she was involved in the mystery of Christianity. A daily terror attended this knowledge, however, for she sensed herself being drawn by that student, that Jewish boy, into a relationship she was not ready for. She wanted to cry out in fear that she was being forced into the role of a Christian, and what did that mean? What could her studies tell her? What could the other nuns tell her? She was alone, no one could help, he was making her into a Christian, and to her that was a mystery, a thing of terror, something others slipped on the way they slipped on their clothes, casually and thoughtlessly, but to her a magnificent and terrifying wonder.

For days she carried Weinstein's paper, marked A,

around with her; he did not come to class. One day she checked with the graduate office and was told that Weinstein had called in to say his father was ill and he would not be able to attend classes for a while. "He's strange, I remember him," the secretary said. "He missed all his exams last spring and made a lot of trouble. He was in and out of here every day."

So there was no more of Weinstein for a while, and Sister Irene stopped expecting him to hurry into class. Then, one morning, she found a letter from him in her mailbox.

He had printed it in black ink, very carefully, as if he had not trusted handwriting. The return address was in bold letters that, like his voice, tried to grab onto her: Birchcrest Manor. Somewhere north of the city. "Dear Sister Irene," the block letters said, "I am doing well here and have time for reading and relaxing. The Manor is delightful. My doctor here is an excellent, intelligent man who has time for me unlike my former doctor. If you have time, you might drop in on my father, who worries about me too much, I think, and explain to him what my condition is. He doesn't seem to understand. I feel about this new life the way that boy, what's his name, in *Measure for Measure,* feels about the prospects of a different life; you remember what he says to his sister when she visits him in prison, how he is looking forward to an escape into another world. Perhaps you could *explain* this to my father and he would stop worrying." The letter ended with the father's name and address, in letters that were just a little too big. Sister Irene, walking slowly down the corridor as she read the letter, felt her eyes cloud over with tears. She was cold with fear, it was something she had never experienced before. She knew what Weinstein was trying to tell her, and the desperation of his attempt made it all the more pathetic; he did not deserve this, why did God allow him to suffer so?

She read through Claudio's speech to his sister, in *Measure for Measure:*

> *Ay, but to die, and go we know not where;*
> *To lie in cold obstruction and to rot;*
> *This sensible warm motion to become*
> *A kneaded clod; and the delighted spirit*
> *To bathe in fiery floods, or to reside*
> *In thrilling region of thicked-ribbèd ice,*
> *To be imprison'd in the viewless winds*
> *And blown with restless violence round about*
> *The pendent world; or to be worse than worst*
> *Of those that lawless and incertain thought*
> *Imagines howling! 'Tis too horrible!*
> *The weariest and most loathèd worldly life*
> *That age, ache, penury, and imprisonment*
> *Can lay on nature is a paradise*
> *To what we fear of death.*

Sister Irene called the father's number that day. "Allen Weinstein residence, who may I say is calling?" a woman said, bored. "May I speak to Mr. Weinstein? It's urgent—about his son," Sister Irene said. There was a pause at the other end. "You want to talk to his mother, maybe?" the woman said. "His mother? Yes, his mother, then. Please. It's very important."

She talked with this strange, unsuspected woman, a disembodied voice that suggested absolutely no face, and insisted upon going over that afternoon. The woman was nervous, but Sister Irene, who was a university professor after all, knew enough to hide her own nervousness. She kept waiting for the woman to say, "Yes, Allen has mentioned you . . ." but nothing happened.

She persuaded Sister Carlotta to ride over with her. This urgency of hers was something they were all amazed by. They hadn't suspected that the set of her gray eyes could change to this blurred, distracted alarm, this sense of mission that seemed to have come to her from nowhere. Sister Irene drove across the city in the late afternoon traffic, with the high whining noises from residential streets where trees were being sawed down in pieces. She understood now the secret, sweet wildness that Christ must have felt, giving himself for man, dying for the billions of men who would never know of him and never understand the sacrifice. For the first time she approached the realization of that great act. In her troubled mind the city traffic was jumbled and yet oddly coherent, an image of the world that was always out of joint with what was happening in it, its inner history struggling with its external spectacle. This sacrifice of Christ's so mysterious and legendary, now almost lost in time—it was that by which Christ transcended both God and man at one moment, more than man because of his fate to do what no other man could do, and more than God because no god could suffer as he did. She felt a flicker of something close to madness.

She drove nervously, uncertainly, afraid of missing the street and afraid of finding it too, for while one part of her rushed forward to confront these people who had betrayed their son, another part of her would have liked nothing so much as to be waiting as usual for the summons to dinner, safe in her room. . . . When she found the street and turned onto it, she was in a state of breathless excitement. Here, lawns were bright green and marred with only a few leaves, magically clean, and the houses were enormous and pompous, a mixture of styles: ranch houses, colonial houses, French country houses, white-bricked wonders with curving glass and clumps of birch trees somehow encircled by white concrete. Sister Irene stared as if she had blundered into another world. This was a kind of heaven, and she was too shabby for it.

The Weinstein's house was the strangest one of all: it looked like a small Alpine lodge, with an inverted-V-shaped front entrance. Sister Irene drove up the black-topped driveway and let the car slow to a stop; she told Sister Carlotta she would not be long.

At the door she was met by Weinstein's mother, a small nervous woman with hands like her son's. "Come in, come in," the woman said. She had once been beautiful, that was clear, but now in missing beauty she was not handsome or even attractive but looked ruined and perplexed, the misshapen swelling of her white-blond professionally set hair like a cap lifting up from her surprised face. "He'll be right in. Allen?" she called, "our visitor is here." They went into the living room. There was a grand piano at one end and an organ at the other. In between were scatterings of brilliant modern furniture, in conversational groups, and several puffed-up white rugs on the polished floor. Sister Irene could not stop shivering. "Professor, it's so strange, but let me say when the phone rang I had a feeling—I had a feeling," the woman said, with damp eyes. Sister Irene sat, and the woman hovered about her. "Should I call you Professor? We don't—you know—we don't understand the technicalities that go with—Allen, my son, wanted to go here to the Catholic school; I told my husband why not? Why fight? It's the thing these days, they do anything they want for knowledge. And he had to come home, you know. He couldn't take care of himself in New York, that was the beginning of the trouble— Should I call you Professor?"

"You can call me Sister Irene."

"Sister Irene?" the woman said, touching her throat in awe, as if something intimate and unexpected had happened.

Then Weinstein's father appeared, hurrying. He took long impatient strides. Sister Irene stared at him and in that instant doubted everything—he was in his fifties, a tall, sharply handsome man, heavy but not fat, holding his shoulders back with what looked like an effort, but holding them back just the same. He wore a dark suit, and his face was flushed, as if he had run a long distance.

"Now," he said, coming to Sister Irene and with a precise wave of his hand motioning his wife off, "now let's straighten this out. A lot of confusion over that kid, eh?" He pulled a chair over, scraping it across a rug and pulling one corner over, so that its brown underside was exposed. "I came home early just for this, Libby phoned me. Sister, you got a letter from him, right?"

The wife looked at Sister Irene over her husband's shoulder as if trying somehow to coach her, knowing that this man was so loud and impatient that no one could remember anything in his presence.

"A letter—yes—today—"

"He says what in it? You got the letter, eh? Can I see it?"

She gave it to him and wanted to explain, but he silenced her with a flick of his hand. He read through the letter so quickly that Sister Irene thought perhaps he was trying to impress her with his skill at reading. "So?" he said, raising his eyes, smiling, "so what is this? He's happy out there, he says. He doesn't communicate with us anymore, but he writes to you and says he's happy—what's that? I mean, what the hell is that?"

"But he isn't happy. He wants to come home," Sister Irene said. It was so important that she make him understand that she could not trust her voice; goaded by this man, it might suddenly turn shrill, as his son's did. "Someone must read their letters before they're mailed, so he tried to tell me something by making an allusion to—"

"What?"

"—an allusion to a play, so that I would know. He might be thinking of suicide, he must be very unhappy—"

She ran out of breath. Weinstein's mother had begun to cry, but the father was shaking his head jerkily back and forth. "Forgive me, Sister, but it's a lot of crap, he needs the hospital, he needs help—right? It costs me fifty a day out there, and they've got the best place in the state, I figure it's worth it. He needs help, that kid, what do I care if he's unhappy? He's unbalanced!" he said angrily. "You want us to get him out again? We argued with the judge for two hours to get him in, an acquaintance of mine. Look, he can't control himself—he was smashing things here, he was hysterical, his room is like an animal was in it. You ever seen anybody hysterical? They need help, lady, and you do something about it fast! You do something! We made up our minds to do something and we did it! This letter—what the hell is this letter? He never talked like that to us!"

"But he means the opposite of what he says—"

"Then he *is* crazy! I'm the first to admit it." He was perspiring, and his face had darkened. "I've got no pride left, this late. He's a little bastard, you want to know? He calls me names, he's filthy, got a filthy mouth—that's being smart, huh? They give him a big scholarship for his filthy mouth? I went to college too, and I got out and knew something, and I for Christ's sake did something with it; my wife is an intelligent woman, a learned woman, would you guess she does book reviews for the little newspaper out here? Intelligent isn't crazy—crazy isn't intelligent— maybe for you at the school he writes nice papers and gets an A, but out here, around the house, he can't control himself, and we got him committed!"

"But—"

"We're fixing him up, don't worry about it!" He turned to his wife. "Libby, get out of here, I mean it. I'm sorry, but get out of here, you're making a fool of yourself, go stand in the kitchen or something, you and the goddamn maid can cry on each other's shoulders. That one in the kitchen is nuts too, they're all nuts. Sister," he said, his voice lowering, "I thank you immensely for coming out here. This is wonderful, your interest in my son. And I see he admired you—that letter there. But what about that letter? If he did want to get out, which I don't admit—he was willing to be committed, in the end he said OK himself—if he wanted out I wouldn't do it. Why? So what if he wants to come back? The next day he wants something else, what then? He's a sick kid, and I'm the first to admit it."

Sister Irene felt that sickness spread to her. She stood. The room was so big that it seemed it must be a public place; there had been nothing personal or private about their conversation. Weinstein's mother was standing by the fireplace, sobbing. The father jumped to his feet and wiped his forehead in a gesture that was meant to help Sister Irene on her way out. "God, what a day," he said, his eyes snatching at hers for understanding, "you know—one of those days all day long? Sister, I thank you a lot. A pro-

fessor interested in him—he's a smart kid, eh? Yes, I thank
you a lot. There should be more people in the world that
care about others, like you. I mean that."

On the way back to the convent, the man's words returned to her, and she could not get control of them; she
could not even feel anger. She had been pressed down,
forced back, what could she do? Weinstein might have
been watching her somehow from a barred window, and he
surely would have understood. The strange idea she had
had on the way over, something about understanding
Christ, came back to her now and sickened her. But the
sickness was small. It could be contained.

About a month after her visit to his father, Weinstein
himself showed up. He was dressed in a suit as before, even
the necktie was the same. He came right into her office as
if he had been pushed and could not stop.

"Sister," he said, and shook her hand. He must have
seen fear in her because he smiled ironically. "Look, I'm
released. I'm let out of the nut house. Can I sit down?"

He sat. Sister Irene was breathing quickly, as if in the
presence of an enemy who does not know that he is an
enemy.

"So, they finally let me out. I heard what you did. You
talked with him, that was all I wanted. You're the only one
who gave a damn. Because you're a humanist and a religious person, you respect . . . the individual. Listen," he
said, whispering, "it was hell out there! Hell! Birchcrest
Manor! All fixed up with fancy chairs and *Life* magazines
lying around—and what do they do to you? They locked
me up, they gave me shock treatments! Shock treatments,
how do you like that, it's discredited by everybody now—
they're crazy out there themselves, sadists—they locked me

up, they gave me hypodermic shots, they didn't treat me like a human being! Do you know what that is," Weinstein demanded savagely, "not to be treated like a human being? They made me an animal—for fifty dollars a day! Dirty filthy swine! Now I'm an outpatient because I stopped swearing at them. I found somebody's bobby pin, and when I wanted to scream I pressed it under my fingernail, and it stopped me—the screaming went inside and not out—so they gave me good reports, those sick bastards, now I'm an outpatient and I can walk along the street and breathe in the same filthy exhaust from the buses like all you normal people! Christ," he said, and threw himself back against the chair.

Sister Irene stared at him. She wanted to take his hand, to make some gesture that would close the aching distance between them. "Mr. Weinstein—"

"Call me Allen!" he said sharply.

"I'm very sorry—I'm terribly sorry—"

"My own parents committed me, but of course they didn't know what it was like. It was hell," he said, thickly, "and there isn't any hell except what other people do to you. The psychiatrist out there, the main shrink, he hates Jews, too, some of us were positive of that, and he's got a bigger nose than I do, a real beak." He made a noise of disgust. "A dirty bastard, a sick, dirty, pathetic bastard— all of them— Anyway, I'm getting out of here, and I came to ask you a favor."

"What do you mean?"

"I'm getting out. I'm leaving. I'm going up to Canada and lose myself, I'll get a job, I'll forget everything, I'll kill myself maybe—what's the difference? Look, can you lend me some money?"

"Money?"

"Just a little! I have to get to the border, I'm going to take a bus."

"But I don't have any money—"

"No money?" He stared at her. "You mean—you don't have any? Sure you have some!"

She stared at him as if he has asked her to do something obscene. Everything was splotched and uncertain before her eyes. "You must . . . you must go back," she said, "you're making a—"

"I'll pay it back. Look, I'll pay it back, can you go to where you live or something and get it? I'm in a hurry. My friends are sons of bitches: one of them pretended he didn't see me yesterday—I stood right in the middle of the sidewalk and yelled at him, I called him some appropriate names! So he didn't see me, huh? You're the only one who understands me, you understand me like a poet, you—"

"I can't help you, I'm sorry—I—"

He looked to one side of her and then flashed his gaze back, as if he could not control it. He seemed to be trying to clear his vision. "You have the soul of a poet," he whispered, "you're the only one. Everybody else is rotten! Can't you lend me some money, ten dollars maybe? I have three thousand in the bank, and I can't touch it! They take everything away from me, they make me into an animal. . . . You know I'm not an animal, don't you? Don't you?"

"Of course," Sister Irene whispered.

"You could get money. Help me. Give me your hand or something, touch me, help me—please—" He reached for her hand and she drew back. He stared at her and his face seemed about to crumble, like a child's. "I want something from you, but I don't know what—I want something!" he cried. "Something real! I want you to look at me like I was a human being, is that too much to ask? I have a brain, I'm alive, I'm suffering—what does that mean? Does that mean nothing? I want something real and not this phony Christian love garbage—it's all in the books, it isn't personal—I want something real—look—"

He tried to take her hand again, and this time she jerked away. She got to her feet. "Mr. Weinstein," she said, "please—"

"You! You—nun," he said scornfully, his mouth twisted into a mock grin. "You nun! There's nothing under that ugly outfit, right? And you're not particularly smart even though you think you are; my father has more brains in his foot than you—"

He got to his feet and kicked the chair.

"You bitch!" he cried.

She shrank back against her desk as if she thought he might hit her, but he only ran out of the office.

Weinstein: the name was to become disembodied from the figure, as time went on. The semester passed, the autumn drizzle turned into snow, Sister Irene rode to school in the morning and left in the afternoon, four days a week, anonymous in her black winter cloak, quiet and stunned. University teaching was an anonymous task, each day dissociated from the rest, with no necessary sense of unity among the teachers: they came and went separately and might for a year just miss a colleague who left his office five minutes before they arrived, and it did not matter.

She heard of Weinstein's death, his suicide by drowning, from the English department secretary, a handsome white-haired woman who kept a transistor radio on her desk. Sister Irene was not surprised; she had been thinking of him as dead for months. "They identified him by some special television way they have now," the secretary said. "They're shipping the body back. It was up in Quebec . . ."

Sister Irene could feel a part of herself drifting off, lured by the plains of white snow to the north, the quiet, the emptiness, the sweep of the Great Lakes up to the silence of Canada. But she called that part of herself back. She could only be one person in her lifetime. That was the ugly truth, she thought, that she could not really regret Weinstein's suffering and death; she had only one life and had already given it to someone else. He had come too late to her. Fifteen years ago, perhaps, but not now.

She was only one person, she thought, walking down the corridor in a dream. Was she safe in this single person, or was she trapped? She had only one identity. She could make only one choice. What she had done or hadn't done was the result of that choice, and how was she guilty? If she could have felt guilt, she thought, she might at least have been able to feel something.

ROUND TRIP
by Charles Healy

On the wall of the convent stairwell, pictures of saints gradually ascended to the second floor or, as the nuns liked to think, to heaven. (Coming *down* the stairs the analogy was suspended.) Sister Rita and Sister Superior stood at the foot of the stairs speaking softly.

"I hope you don't mind going, Sister," Sister Superior said. "We could order the books by mail, but she loves to get out once in a while."

"That's all right, Sister. I really don't mind."

Sister Raphael appeared at the top of the stairs carrying an umbrella and an empty, wrinkled shopping bag. When she saw the Superior she stepped back out of sight, but it was too late.

"I don't think that's a good idea, Sister," Sister Superior called up the stairs.

Sister Raphael poked her head over the banister. "What isn't, Sister?"

"The white shoes."

"White shoes?"

"Yes, Sister." The Superior nodded at what looked like a white mouse peeking around the base of the banister post. When Sister Raphael looked down it darted out of sight.

"They're very cool," Sister Raphael said absently, looking at the spot where her foot had been. Then, looking down at the two nuns, "They have tiny air holes, you know." But there wasn't any fight in her voice and after a few moments she disappeared.

"She's always trying to slip out with those on," Sister

113

Superior said. "They're from the time she was stationed at the hospital, St. Clair's. She doesn't realize they look all right with the white habit, but they look silly with the black."

Sister Rita, who didn't look that old, went, "Tsk, tsk."

"I told her if she likes them so much she should dye them black, but of course she won't. She says the dye would block the air holes so her feet can't breathe."

"Isn't that something," Sister Rita said, shaking her head. "The poor thing."

Upon hearing Sister Raphael's cell door open and close, the Superior gave a little wave and moved away. When Raphael came down, she and Rita made a brief visit to the chapel, then went to the front door. Rita removed the chain and the bolt while Raphael impeded as much by her umbrella, shopping bag and Little Office as by old age, was still fumbling with the key. Outside, they walked to Mr. Ryan's car which was double-parked in front of the convent.

Whenever he was angry or upset, Mr. Ryan's lower jaw stuck out like a car ash tray. Now, waiting for the nuns, his jaw was out far enough to accommodate a fat stogie. Several months before, he had picked up Sister Raphael and a younger nun uptown and given them a ride back to the convent. He had always thought that nuns were only allowed out to visit the sick or attend funerals, so he hadn't foreseen any danger in inviting them to call on him anytime they needed a ride. And that's when the dam burst. He couldn't begin to estimate how many miles he had logged since then with a carful of nuns. Especially that old one. She seemed to spend more time out than in. (And Mr. Ryan suspected that all her trips weren't on the up-and-up. Once she had called him and, in a whisper, was telling him when to pick her up. Suddenly she said, "I can't talk now," and hung up.) She seemed to Mr. Ryan like a child who would run until she dropped and he imagined one of the nuns tucking her in ("Nightnight!") while she, wearing a bonnet like one of those plastic dish covers, looked up bright-eyed from her pillow, ready to leap out of bed the moment the other nun left the room.

She was a sketch all right. Her and those beads. If he jumped a light or cut in too soon, she'd pipe up, "Shall we say a rosary, Sisters, for a safe trip?"

They'd cost him money too. Mr. Ryan had an appliance store, and he figured it would be good for business if word got around that he had given the nuns a couple of items at cost. Well, before they were through they'd gotten a refrigerator, a freezer and half a dozen window fans. Mr. Ryan looked ruefully up at the convent. With two of his largest fans slowly spinning in the parlor windows, it looked like a Victorian houseboat run aground. When he remembered how much he would have made on them retail, he looked away and so didn't see the two nuns as they came out.

"Good afternoon, Mr. Ryan," Sister Rita said as she opened the back door. Mr. Ryan started to get out, but Sister Rita told him to stay put because he was double-parked (Was that a crack?) and would have to step into traffic. "And we don't want to lose our favorite chauffeur." Ordinarily Mr. Ryan would have gotten out anyway, but the pants he had on were so small that the zipper showed in a toothy V just below his shirt. He closed his door and sat back.

Rita got in first so that Raphael would not have to climb to the far side of the car. But when she sat down she saw that the older nun was already settled in the front seat and rolling down the window. Rita moved back to the other side, closed the door, and sat down with a sigh. In front of her, Raphael's head, a small, smooth melon under the black veil, barely showed above the seat. Rita wondered idly if Raphael could even see out the window.

"Ground chuck, two pounds, eighty-nine cents," Raphael called out, reading a sign in the A&P window. "We'll have to tell Sister Irma about that, Sister."

"Yes, Sister," Sister Rita answered, but the car and Sister Raphael had already gone on to something else.

"Donleavey's Bar and Grill. Tables for Ladies." Raphael turned her head so that Rita could see her profile through the side of her veil. With all signs of femininity gone from her face, she might have been a priest hearing confessions. "I wonder if that could be the Donleavey boy in your class, Sister."

Rita hadn't known before that Danny Donleavey's father owned a tavern. But she had once asked the children to bring in dust cloths for washing down the blackboard and Danny had brought in a blue-checked table cloth. The table cloth was like new so that rather than tear it up for dust rags, Rita had used it on the May altar—a table at the rear of the classroom which held a statue of the Blessed Mother and was decked with flowers for the month of May. The table cloth was just like those Rita saw on the Tables for Ladies, and she bit her lip as she remembered her remark as she had smoothed the cloth around the statue. "Isn't that lovely, children? And it's blue, Our Lady's color."

Our Lady's color! "I don't know, Sister," she said.

While Raphael continued to read signs aloud, Rita found herself frowning at the statues of St. Patrick and St. Francis on the dashboard. She had disapproved of them from the first time she saw one. ("It's St. Christopher,"

Raphael had said, attaching the statue to the radiator at a hazardous angle. "He has a magnetic bottom.") Rita preferred her saints in a setting of candlelight and stained glass —not windshield wipers and oncoming traffic—but she kept her opinion to herself when she learned that the Bishop not only approved of them but was something of a collector. Anxious not to offend any nationality, His Excellency had a standing order for one of every statue produced. The dashboard of his Fleetwood now looked like a mob scene from a biblical movie, and Father O'Bannion insisted that he had spotted Charlton Heston in the crowd.

They were passing a block which was completely torn down for redevelopment, so Raphael turned her attention to Mr. Ryan.

"How's that special intention coming?"

"Pardon, Sister?"

"That special intention you wanted me to pray for."

"Oh, that. Fine, Sister."

Rita turned quickly to the window. The test of her Christian charity was never greater than when Raphael got on the subject of special intentions, and she was afraid that if Mr. Ryan caught her eye in the rear-view mirror (he seemed to be trying to make contact everytime Raphael said something), she would go smiling over to the enemy.

Wherever she went, Raphael distributed prayers like tips. If a waitress or sales clerk was particularly attentive, she would ask if they had a special intention they'd like her to pray for. Of course, it's common practice for people to ask nuns to pray for them. But it's also common practice for nuns simply to make the intention to add that person to their prayers and let it go at that. But not Raphael. Once someone agreed that, Yes, there was something she might pray for, Raphael wondered aloud if they didn't want to tell her exactly what the intention was. Her tone insinuated that this information would help her to pipe the request through the proper channels—St. Christopher for the safe return of a loved one, St. Jude for hopeless cases ("Of course, I'm not making any promises").

Rita was happy to see that most people denied Raphael this information, claiming that special intentions, like wishes, must be kept secret to come true. (One sad exception was a book store clerk who, under pressure from Raphael, admitted that his marriage was in trouble because he was impotent. Fortunately, Raphael thought impotence had something to do with being retarded and came away saying, "He seemed intelligent enough to me.") Rita was certain that many of these people didn't really have any intention in mind and were just being nice to Raphael. And, although she knew there must be a kind of celestial clearing house to reroute such pointless prayers to the Poor Souls in Purgatory, it depressed her to think how many of Raphael's prayers, like the dime given for coffee and spent on drink, were sent aloft for fictitious causes. She imagined a heavenly clerk frowning over a scrap of parchment and calling out, "Anybody got anything on a Mrs. Dixon, runs a religious supply store?"

And another thing: Raphael, in a misguided sense of humility, seemed to have put an exact limit on just how many intentions she could take on before her effectiveness as an intermediary suffered. Thus, someone who casually asked her to pray for a sick aunt, would be checked periodically to see if the aunt had died or mended sufficiently to be taken off Raphael's danger list.

"Did you get it?" Raphael asked Mr. Ryan.

"Get what, Sister?"

"What I was praying for."

"Oh. Yes. Yes, I did."

"Good." Raphael reached into her pocket, brought out a small notebook, then took a lead pencil out of a holster on her belt. She opened the notebook and started to make a mark. Then she paused and looked at Mr. Ryan.

"Is there anything else?"

"Pardon, Sister?"

"Do you want me to pray for something else?"

"No, thank you, Sister."

"No special intentions?"

"I don't think so, Sister."

Raphael nodded, made a mark in the book (presumably through Mr. Ryan's name), then wrote something directly under it.

My Lord! Sister Rita thought, she has a waiting list.

"Tom and Jerry's Newsstand," Raphael called out as she put the pad and pencil away. "That's where Monsignor gets his papers." Then, looking at Mr. Ryan, she added, "They deliver." Rita wasn't sure whether this was added to assure Mr. Ryan that Monsignor had more important things to do than to go out for the papers or to feed the rumor that Monsignor hadn't been out of the rectory in ten years.

The car crawled to a traffic light. As the light turned orange, Mr. Ryan threw the car into second gear and cut left across the intersection before the oncoming traffic knew what hit it. A teen-age boy in a two-tone Ford tried to beat him out but, with the extra weight of a spotlight, fog lights and a plump girl who seemed absorbed with something going on inside his ear, he had to settle for leaning on his horn as he cut through Mr. Ryan's wake. Mr. Ryan, flushed with victory, saw that Sister Raphael had snatched at the beads hanging from her belt.

"Don't worry, Sister," Mr. Ryan said, waving a hand at the statues on the dashboard. "My little saints take care of me."

"They're not watching the road either," Raphael snapped back.

Rita decided to change the subject before Raphael could utter any further blasphemies. She asked Mr. Ryan how his family was, although she knew that he was one of those people who took such questions literally: Mrs. Ryan was fine (apparently over that "woman trouble" he had told them about last time); Jeff's trick knee, an old football injury, was kicking up again; Marie was over her cold (but must have passed it on to him because he woke up this morning with the sniffles); and last but not least, little Annie was checking in St. Mary's next day to have her tonsils out.

By this time they had pulled up to the station and Raphael was on the edge of her seat, anxiously watching the train that had just pulled in. "We'll pray for a speedy recovery or happy death," she said as she stepped out of the car and headed for the station.

Rita hated to leave Mr. Ryan like that, but if she didn't hurry, Raphael, to her delight, would be on the train alone.

On the train, Rita put their tickets in the slot on the seat, but Raphael retrieved them.

"I want to see something," she said, putting the tickets in her pocket.

Raphael's habit, even as habits go, was large. The sleeves were very long (although they still managed to be half an inch shorter than the sleeves of her underwear), and the veil jutted far out around her face like a shadow box. Her face did not fill the coif so that when she turned

her head the side jackknifed, revealing one of her very
large ears. Raphael had been Rita's teacher in grammar
school and in those days her coif had been as tight as a
bathing cap, so Rita sometimes wondered whether this was
a new habit or if, with advancing age, the old nun was
shrinking up inside it. (She remembered with some guilt
that she had made this observation a few nights ago in the
community room and had gotten quite a laugh with the
suggestion that, if Raphael lived long enough, she would
disappear from sight altogether, her voice coming back to
them as if from a well.) The overall effect was that Raphael
lived in the habit rather than wore it.

When the conductor stopped and asked for their tickets,
Rita nodded towards Sister Raphael who was staring
straight ahead.

"Tickets, please," the conductor repeated.

Raphael continued to stare ahead.

"Tickets, please."

Still nothing.

"Tickets, please."

The conductor seemed prepared to wait until doomsday
so Raphael played her trump card. She closed her eyes and
began to move her lips, supposedly in prayer.

The conductor bent over and whispered very reverently,
"Tickets, please."

Rita would have let the two of them fight it out if there
was some way she could give the other passengers the impression that she, Rita, by special permission from the
Mother House, was traveling alone and, by some incredible coincidence, had landed next to another solitary nun
who, though from the same order as Rita, was a total
stranger to her. Failing that, Rita laid her hand on Raphael's arm. "*Sister!* the tickets." Raphael looked at her

and nodded, then thrust one arm into her pocket up to the elbow. Dying hard, she thrashed about in her pocket for a while before producing the tickets and turning them over to the conductor.

As the conductor moved away, Raphael poked Rita with her elbow. "He must be a left-hander," she whispered. "But he looked as Irish as Paddy's pig." She shook her head wonderingly. "The last one's name was O'Brien, and he said we shouldn't even have bought tickets."

Rita, who didn't believe in trainmen giving out free rides on trains which were not their personal property, was glad the conductor had persevered. She opened her Little Office and had just started to read when Raphael jabbed her in the ribs again, "Maybe we'll get one of our own on the way back," she said in a whisper that could be heard half-way down the car.

In the Grand Central tunnel, the train inexplicably slowed and stopped several times, as if cows were crossing the tracks. Finally, the platform slid up to the train, and the two nuns, at Raphael's signal, stood up. Raphael took the lead and staggered down the aisle. She stopped a few inches from the door and stood staring at the glass as if waiting for her reflection to stand aside. When the conductor came through she followed him out of the car, and when he opened the outside door, she stood in the opening like a paratrooper, squinting into the wind. Rita, though the platform rushing by made her nervous, stood close behind Raphael in case she tried to step off before they reached the jump zone.

Sister Raphael seemed to know her way around Grand Central. She indicated some escalators, which had not been there the last time Sister Rita was in New York, and started towards them. Halfway there, her head jerked around and her hand shot up under her wimple. Rita caught her breath; at Raphael's age it could just as well be her heart as her watch. But it was her watch, which she checked against the huge clock across the station. As she replaced the watch in the small pocket on her breast, her wimple lifted, revealing the usual nun's jewelry: a scattering of common pins, one or two safety pins, one sewing needle flying its banner of black thread, and a Sacred Heart badge.

As soon as Raphael boarded the escalator she braced herself to get off. She stood facing square ahead, feet flat and elbows out so that the umbrella and shopping bag were clear. As she approached the top she went into a slight crouch and up on her toes, then was propelled forward, taking quick little steps to catch up with herself, like a vaudeville comedian pretending to have been pushed on-stage. When they were on their way again, Raphael shook her head and said, "A person could get killed on one of those things." But it was clear from her expression that she considered it a beautiful way to go.

They went directly to a book store on Fifth Avenue and ordered some books for the school. When they came out Rita tried to steer Raphael back towards Grand Central. Instead, Raphael took Rita on a tour of five-and-ten cent stores and in each one managed to become separated from the younger nun. At first, Rita thought these separations were accidental, but when she realized how long it took them to find each other, she began to suspect that she was the only one looking. Her suspicions were confirmed when, after they were reunited in the bowels of Lamston's hardware department, she saw that Raphael's shopping bag had begun to balloon.

Her first thought was that the old nun had been taking things unconsciously or naively, thinking everything was free for nuns. For a moment she considered turning her in, but the resulting scene which she imagined taking place in the manager's office dissuaded her: After explaining to the manager and the store detective that Raphael was like a child, really, and didn't mean any harm, the detective snarled, "We've heard that one before, lady." Then, sticking his cold cigar into his mouth to get it out of the way, he walked across the room and roughly raised Raphael's habit. There, in the folds of her petticoat, hung pots, pans, composition books, a pump action flit gun, a Japanese fan and other five-and-ten treasures. The scene seemed so real to Rita that, as they left the store she caught herself listening to hear whether Raphael clanked when she walked. She didn't. She jingled.

So she had money. And God knows how many cadged taxi, train and bus rides it represented. Even if she hadn't caught a glimpse of the red cab of a toy truck, Rita should have known that the bag was filled with toys. And, even though she knew there was something in there earmarked for *her* nephew, she felt irritated. Why should Raphael have money to throw away while the rest of the nuns cut the signatures off Christmas cards received and sent them out the following years as their own? Why should Raphael have money to spend on things like the new umbrella she was carrying while the other nuns hung their patched underwear on the line inside pillowcases, a flapping chorus for Raphael's longjohns?

Apparently Raphael had done all the shopping she wanted to do because Rita now had little trouble getting her back to Grand Central and onto a train. Raphael grabbed the window seat and put the shopping bag between her legs. Rita offered to put the bag up in the rack.

"What shopping bag?" Raphael asked, snapping her legs together so that all that showed were the two loop-like handles. They looked like grips placed there so that the old nun could be picked up. And Rita felt like doing just that —picking Raphael up and giving her a good shaking. Instead she sat and brooded over the humiliation the contents of the shopping bag promised for the next visiting Sunday.

Visiting Days at the convent were hard on the children who were dragged along. There were no knickknacks to distract them (all the statues were symbolically out of reach), and their parents, intimidated perhaps by the murky oil paintings of heaven's citizens looking down their noses from every wall, never brought any toys along.

Rita did not blame the children for being restless and depressed. When she was first assigned to St. John's she felt the same way. The furniture was thick and angular and no two pieces seemed to be related, so that, looking around the room, her eye bumped along like a stick on a picket fence. What's more, the rooms were very high and so poorly lighted that it always seemed about to rain inside. Anyway, when the long afternoon began to tell on the children, and they seemed on the verge of climbing down from the chairs and running amuck in the wide, polished corridors, the nun whom they were visiting would bring out small gifts wrapped in tissue paper and tied with plain string.

These gifts were necessarily make-do affairs—odd items found around the convent, or gifts the nuns themselves had received. But they all had two things in common. First, they were religious (Lay people, in despair over what you can possibly give to a nun, invariably settle on the one thing she has enough of.) Second, they were imperfect, for any articles in mint condition were displayed in a tall china closet, its dwarf legs buckling under the weight of statues, missals and crucifixes. The closet was located in the main corridor, and the nuns were encouraged to steer visitors by it, mentioning in passing that the articles were for sale. (In doing this, Sister Rita always watched visitors' faces self-consciously for a flicker of recognition.)

Whatever enthusiasm was aroused by the appearance of the presents always fell off drastically when they were un-wrapped, and in a few minutes the children would be squirming and whining again. At that point (had she been at the keyhole?) Raphael would poke her head in the door, make a quick head count, then disappear. A few minutes later she would return with an armful of gaily wrapped packages. There were yo-yos, tops, noise-makers, model airplanes and so on, and the children immediately forgot that, seconds before, they were crying to go bye-bye.

Rita frankly resented Raphael's interference in her visits. Her chances to ingratiate herself with her nephews were few (they came so seldom that a good part of the afternoon was spent getting them over their fear of the habit), so it was annoying to know that the high point of their visit was Sister Raphael's appearance. And if it wasn't for Rita's groundwork, the old nun would have been as welcome as the bogeymen, presents or no. Then, too, Rita knew that her sister and brother-in-law must wonder why she gave the children religious articles (and rejects at that) while old

Sister What's-her-name went all out. Rita sometimes wondered if the reason they seldom brought the children was because George (who didn't go to Mass at all before Betty married him and now stayed awake only long enough to pick out something in the sermon to criticize) figured she was vocation hunting. In charity, of course, Rita couldn't explain the situation. So, as she sat grimly watching the children playing with Raphael's presents (and with Raphael herself, who got right down on the floor with them), she imagined the graces flowing into her soul like plasma. Somehow—and this worried her—it was a small consolation.

Rita interrupted her reflections when she became aware that the train was in a station and Raphael was twisting around in the seat, her face quite close to the window. A woman and three children on the platform seemed to be laughing and waving at Raphael so Rita leaned forward to see what was going on. She saw that Raphael was playing a child's game, pressing her face against the window until her nose and lips were bloodless blurbs. Before Rita could duck back, one of the children shouted, "There's another one!" Pressing back in her seat, Rita picked up where she had left off.

She remembered the time she went to see Sister Superior and told her that she was troubled by her attitude towards Sister Raphael. Sister Superior pooh-poohed Rita's idea that her feelings were sinful and admitted that on at least two occasions she herself had come within an inch of sending Raphael off to St. Agnes'—the rest home where the old nuns who are no longer useful in the classroom sit around listening to the dimming sound of clapping erasers and greeting their rare visitors with, "Where's your homework?"

"What happened?" Rita had asked, feeling better already.

The superior told how she had found Raphael holding a string of luminous beads to the window as if to a crowd kneeling on the front lawn. When she asked what she was doing, Raphael had said, "Recharging them."

"And do you remember the time Sister Charlotte's relatives from California stopped to see her?" Sister Superior had gone on. "They were going to the World's Fair, and were to have started back again before Visiting Sunday, so I told her it was all right if they stopped. All her family lives so far away she only gets visitors about once a year anyway. Later, I dropped in St. Joseph's parlor to say hello, and Sister Raphael came in with a tray of tea and soda and cookies. And you remember Sister Charlotte's niece, the one about three?"

"Yes, she was very cute."

"Well, she looked up at the picture of the Bishop, the big one of him in his ermine cap and lace surplice, and she pointed at it and said, "Lady!"

Rita caught her breath as Sister Superior paused. She could tell from her expression there was more to come.

"Then," the Superior went on, "before anyone could correct the child, Sister Raphael said, "Yes, see the nice lady!"

After that, as if Sister Superior had passed the word, other nuns had volunteered stories about Raphael. Sister Matthew, for example, told of the time that her brother-in-law, a former pupil of Raphael's was about to go into the visitor's lavatory when Raphael came along with another nun. "I remember when you had to have my permission to go in there," she called out.

Sister Mary Clement told about the day she and Raphael were talking to Father O'Bannion in the schoolyard. Just for something to say, Father pointed to a window on the second floor of the rectory and said, "That's my room."

"What are you telling us for?" Raphael said, cackling wildly.

And, of course, it was no secret that Mother General avoided meeting Raphael whenever possible, especially when lay people were around. It seems that, before her election, it was the custom for the nuns to keep their family names. However, when Sister Hubbard became Mother Hubbard, she quickly pushed through an amendment (retroactive) whereby the nuns would take a Saint's name at profession. (Those parents who objected to the fact that their daughters would not retain their family name could take some consolation in the knowledge that the change was inevitable: Sister Michael Peter, the former Mary McCree of the Waterbury McCrees, was a sure bet to succeed the present Mother General). Raphael, however, had never been able to adjust to the change and still called all the old-timers by their family names. So, at the annual bazaar held on the grounds of the novitiate, if you saw Mother General or Sister Thomas (nee Gladys Lipshitz) or Sister Estelle (nee Mary Twitty) ducking behind a bush or disappearing around a corner, you could be pretty sure that Raphael was pursuing in full call.

Although some of the nuns laughed when they told these stories, Rita knew that they were not simply amused by Sister Raphael's antics. The nuns knew too well that lay people tend to reason from the particular to the general ("Whatever you do, don't send your kid to a Catholic school. Why, I knew this nun once . . ."), so each felt a responsibility to every nun everywhere in her dealings with the outside world. Therefore it wasn't simply that Raphael didn't present the best face to the world, but, with her unique ability to get out of the convent on all kinds of spurious errands, she presented that face all too often.

When they got off the train, Raphael finally seemed to be tiring. But even as she walked slowly along she looked all about for some diversion. Rita, walking at her elbow, urging her along, felt as though she were carrying a split grocery bag, trying to get home before something fell out.

As the turned toward the corner where Mr. Ryan was to meet them, Raphael stopped and grabbed Rita by the arm.

"Sister! Look!" she said, pointing to a man lying on the sidewalk to the right of them. He was heavy, middle-aged and wore dark, rumpled clothing. His eyes were closed and his lips were moving as if he were trying to eat something without tasting it.

"He must be drunk," Rita said. She took a suggestive step toward the corner, but Raphael had already started over to the man. Rita wanted to keep on going, but knew she couldn't leave Raphael alone. And so she stood fretting, several yards away, a crowd of one giving him air.

Raphael crouched down next to the man, her umbrella slanting out from her side like a sword. She let go of her shopping bag and, after teetering for a few seconds, it toppled over, spilling some of its contents. A small car with a one-dimensional man at the wheel buzzed across the sidewalk toward Rita but ran down before it reached her. Raphael leaned close to the man.

"Can I help you?" she asked as calmly as if she were answering the door at the convent. The man moaned and his lips bubbled. Raphael leaned closer. "Are you a

Catholic?" He moaned again, and his hands opened and closed at his sides. Rita shivered, hearing his nails scratch the pavement.

Suddenly the man started to breathe in great gasps, and his chest rose and fell violently. Raphael got down on her hands and knees and put her mouth close to his ear. "Make an Act of Contrition!" she shouted. "Tell God you're sorry!" The man's head and feet lifted at the same time, a fish curving on land. He gave another loud groan and at the height of it he seemed to shape it into a crude, "God!" Then he fell back and his head cracked against the pavement. A few moments later his closed fists relaxed.

When the ambulance arrived, the doctor started to examine the man while the driver went to the back of the ambulance to get the oxygen tank. When the driver walked over with the tank, the doctor told him to put it back and bring the stretcher.

As she watched them put the man on the stretcher, Rita wondered about the man's cry. It might have been an exclamation or a curse, but suppose it was a prayer. Since we are responsible for any sins we commit while drunk, because we are responsible for getting drunk in the first place, what about prayers said while we're drunk? It would seem that we're responsible for those too. So the man might have saved his soul without knowing it. It was an interesting question, but she put it out of her mind when she pictured the man staggering into heaven scratching his stomach and mumbling, "Where the hell am I?"

The doctor started to cover the man's face with a blanket but, after glancing at the crowd, stopped it at his chest. As they lifted the stretcher into the ambulance, Raphael walked next to it smoothing the blanket.

"That's all right, Sister," the doctor said. "He's dead."

"Yes," Raphael said absently as she brushed away another wrinkle.

By the time they got back to the convent the nuns were already at supper, so Rita didn't see Sister Superior alone until the next morning.

"Did everything go all right yesterday?" Sister Superior asked after holding Rita in the corridor until the rest of the nuns had filed into chapel.

"Yes, Sister. Fine."

"I hope she wasn't too much trouble."

"I didn't mind, Sister. She enjoys it so."

"I know," Sister Superior said and placed her hand on Rita's arm. "I have to go to New York in a few weeks myself. I'll take you as my partner."

"Thank you, Sister. I'd like that."

They were interrupted by a clicking of beads.

"There you are," Raphael said, coming out of the chapel. "I thought you both died in your sleep."

She was about to say something else when a bell sounded, and they heard the nuns in chapel getting to their feet. Sister Raphael, whose voice always got away from her when she tried to whisper, said, "There's the bell!" Rita saw two boxers rushing to the center of the ring.

As slow as she was, Raphael was back in her seat before Rita and the Superior had even entered the chapel. It was almost as though they didn't want anyone to think they were with her.

THE MODEL CHAPEL
by Madeline De Frees

All the nuns seemed to think that the plastic pigs were a wonderful idea. Sister Jude, the bursar, came home from the bank one September morning with a paper bag full of them and set them out on the community room table in three rows—red, yellow, and green—with *Lincoln First Federal Savings & Loan* stamped on their fat sides.

"Now!' she said, picking up a red pig and setting it a little apart from the others, "maybe our novena will work faster." She giggled and looked around at the other Sisters, her eye coming to rest on Sister Constance with a calculated gleam. "Sister Constance can write a little poem to put on the banks, can't she, Sister Superior?" Sister Jude asked. "You know, something to let people know what they're for."

Sister Constance groaned. Even after twenty years she loathed these impromptu orders for verse. (They always called them poems, of course.) In the novitiate it had been different. Everybody wrote jingles there, as if rhyme were the only language audible in that rarefied atmosphere. But in a college, supposedly peopled by adults, it was like using a fountain pen to dig worms.

Sister Superior sent a mischievous look in the direction of Sister Constance, who instantly felt childish and ashamed. "Maybe you can do something in the Edgar Guest tradition," she suggested, and Sister Constance felt her amusement even as she warmed to her sympathy.

In the end Sister Constance had escaped writing the jingle. She had intended to, really, but the bursar was in a hurry and Sister Marian, head of the music department, comprehending the urgency of the situation, had responded. She had seemed eager to demonstrate that art was in no way inconsistent with the practical, even if certain people stubbornly took that view.

Sister Constance had learned, on the other hand, that nuns are people and that, among them, inconsistencies turned up in about the same proportions as elsewhere. If the inconsistencies showed more at times, well, that was because nuns lived so close together.

So now the pigs were being fattened for market. There was a red one on the table in the tiny reception room beside the front entrance of the administration building. Its yellow counterpart stood in the dim recesses of the room across the entry, just beneath the ornate gold-framed Fra Angelico angels. Each morning after breakfast, Sister Jude stopped in the parlor on her way to the novena and opened the venetian blinds enough to frame the pig in a pool of sunlight, but Sister Clare, whose charge it was to dust the parlors, always closed the blinds when Sister Jude was out of sight.

The other eight banks were distributed at strategic points throughout the house, in areas open to visitors and students: one in the bursar's office, one on the cafeteria counter, three in the music room (Sister Constance didn't know whether music students were three times as responsive or triply resistant), one in an obscure corner of the president's office, one in the library, and one, green and animal, at the very feet of the statue of Our Lady of Fatima in the main hall. On one side of each of them, Scotch-taped over the bank imprint, was a small typed message: "A fervent prayer/ An extra penny/ For our new chapel/ To sanctify many." Sister Constance still cringed at the sight of it.

She went to the novena, though, every morning except Tuesday, when it was her turn to do the breakfast dishes. Several of the nuns remained stubbornly away, preferring their private prayer to the choral recitation of one honoring the Infant Jesus of Prague. But Sister Constance, whose reservations about the devotion were equally strong, yielded her judgment and offered the sacrifice of seeming concurrence. She would enter the chapel, genuflect slowly, bow her head in silent adoration and recite the words mechanically. When her eye fell on the dressed-up doll with the crown of gilt and pearls, that took the place of a real statue of the Infant in their tiny chapel, she was sometimes moved to genuine prayer—but it was prayer of atonement and not of petition.

As a young nun, she might have felt obliged to muffle her distaste for cheap religious art. Now she knew that God does not demand suspension of the critical faculties; that obedience and intelligence, taste even, can be reconciled without compromise. Yet it was difficult to apply the principle in particular cases.

Her reaction bothered her sometimes, it seemed so pharisaical. After all, there was something beautiful about the faith and fervor of her Sisters: they were so positive that the Infant could not refuse a petition obviously in accord with the Divine Will. What could more evidently be for God's glory than a new chapel? Their present one was too small entirely and hardly a fitting House for the Divine Guest. When they had outgrown the original chapel, they had removed the sliding doors between it and the community room, moved the altar from the east wall to the south and turned the *prie-dieu* to face it. Gradually they had added more of the tiny kneelers until the whole recess about the Wurlitzer organ was filled with them, and the junior Sisters, turned sideways in the alcove that had once housed the altar, were scarcely three feet from the priest as he offered Mass.

There was no Communion railing either, and two Sisters had to leave the chapel, carrying their chairs, and wait in the hall if one of the nuns wanted to go to Confession before morning Mass.

Sister Constance's place was in the second row at the side, wedged between Sister Catherine and the small niche for the Blessed Mother's statue. Sometimes on feast days the sacristan moved the statue to a pedestal in front of the chapel, where it belonged really, and Sister Constance used the shelf for her hymn books and prayer books. That was why she liked the place, even though she sometimes jabbed her left arm on the base of the niche when someone moved the kneelers a fraction and disturbed their alignment. Yes, a new chapel would be a great convenience, and it was something to pray and suffer for, but not too eagerly, for Sister Constance had learned that so long as a thing matters too much, nothing comes of it.

So she continued to attend the novena, all through the fall, and by November she took one of the plastic pigs from the music room and perched it on a filing case in her classroom. She removed the verse, though, substituting a small notation which read, "How about a dime? I'm building a chapel."

It seemed more honest and more direct; for though she could muster little enthusiasm for Walt Disney cartoons and talking animals generally, the message did avoid the trap of confusing piety and fund-raising.

Sister Constance couldn't help noting, though, that the direct approach seemed less effective. While two or three coins rattled forlornly in her bank, Sister Marian's had already been downtown and back for a refill several times. Once or twice, there had been a dollar bill among the nickels and pennies and quarters; and the bank balance, padded out with a couple of checks from Sister Marian's friends and the proceeds from the sale of some scrap metal, now stood at an impressive $323.89.

It would take at least fifty thousand before they could start, Sister Superior said. But even at the present rate, there could be a new chapel in about eighty years—hardly a long time in the light of eternity, as Sister Jude was at pains to point out. And that would be entirely apart from the novena, which might, at any instant, produce a miracle. Not that they were looking for something extraordinary, you understand, just the softening of an indifferent or hardened heart with purse strings conveniently attached. Didn't the Jesuits experience things like that almost every week? And weren't the Sisters entitled to some mark of Divine favor? After all, Our Lord had urged His followers to ask and they should receive.

Sister Constance wanted to remind Sister Jude that He had also chosen a stable as His birthplace and Nazareth for a home town, but she thought better of it and continued to attend the novena.

Early in December, Sister Jude brought another surprise to the community recreation. The Sisters were sitting around darning their stockings, crocheting or playing Scrabble when Sister Jude walked in with a large carton, which she deposited squarely in front of Sister Superior. There was a rustle of curiosity, and the voices trailed off as Sister Superior rapped with her ring on the table for attention. Sister Jude opened the carton slowly, pushing each flap out of the way and then looking round as if to ask, "Do they really deserve to see this exquisite thing that I have brought them?"

After the carton was undone, there was tissue paper. Sister Jude removed it carefully, piece by piece, smoothing each one out and folding it neatly in four before taking another.

Her timing is all off, Sister Constance thought, as Sister Clare and Sister Timothy went wordlessly back to their Scrabble. Even the sacristan, who might have guessed that it would have something to do with the chapel, stopped looking at Sister Jude and returned to her mending with that terrible concentration known only to those newly fitted with bifocals.

By that time even Sister Jude realized that the game was up, so she cleared her throat and said, "Mr. Henry A. Madison, of Madison & Caldwell, has prepared a scale model of our chapel for display purposes." She reached into the box, took it out, and held it aloft for the Sisters' admiration.

When everyone had exclaimed sufficiently and had examined it at close range, the whole community straggled to the parlor, where the model chapel was enshrined beside the piggy bank. The pig, Sister Constance noted, was not in scale. Its yellow bulk, fully two inches above the clerestory, interposed an earthy barrier between the beholder and the concave shaft from which rose a slim, modernistic cross. The architect had remembered everything: there was a small flashlight battery attached, and when you pushed a switch on the green cork lawn, light streamed through the tiny stained-glass windows in a blue and mystic haze. The Sisters never stopped marveling at the perfection of it, and ten days later the battery had gone dead, though the novena had been thoroughly recharged, and even Sister Clare, who had at first referred to the morning chapel goers as Holy Rollers, now stopped ducking into the parlor to close the venetian blinds and went, instead, to her place in the third row behind Sister Constance.

Seeing the model chapel was certain to draw questions from visitors, the Sisters agreed, and who could tell when the Little King might send a millionaire—one looking for just such an opportunity on which to lavish a fraction of his wealth?

But as day followed day and no benefactor appeared, the novena thinned out a little. Oh no! they had not lost faith nor relinquished hope; it was just that activities multiplied as the school year continued, and some found their early-morning duties too urgent to leave time for spiritual extras.

So the scale model began to disappear into the other indistinguishable features of the reception room until one day when a newspaper reporter spied it, as he was coming in on another assignment. The inevitable questions drew the inevitable answers, and when he asked to do a story and use a picture, Sister Superior reluctantly consented, after making it clear that plans were still tentative and that no date had been set for starting construction. "But," as she remarked, "you never know who might read the story. Remember the nuns in the Old Folks' Home in Kentucky? They had been praying to St. Joseph for a new furnace, and a single news item brought them more than enough donations to pay for the project."

So the story appeared—a fine, inspiring account with a modest, two-column headline and a dignified photograph of Sister Superior examining the architect's model. But days passed, and the only communication elicited by the newspaper story was a frosty reprimand from the provincial superior, who wrote that she had "read with interest of your building program in the public press."

A few days later, Sister Superior and Sister Jude put the model chapel away in the parlor cupboard. The pig now presided over a heavy glass ashtray, the single concession to outsiders in the stiff, airless room with nothing to look at but a plastic-covered pamphlet containing the encyclical on Christian education and a finger-marked copy of last season's college yearbook.

By springtime the nuns were convinced that the Little King was testing their perseverance. St. Monica had prayed twenty or thirty years for Augustine's conversion, and who were they to presume? Of course they must do their part—supplement prayer with whatever action seemed advisable, for Christ had also said, hadn't He, that they must be wise as serpents?

Sister Jude reminded the Sisters at supper one evening that Mrs. McKinstry, a graduate of the normal school and widow of their good friend, might be approached for help. "Why don't we offer our regular novena with special fervor for nine days," she asked, "and then invite her over and propose a memorial chapel?"

It seemed like a direct inspiration, and fervor flared again in the little chapel each morning after breakfast. On the ninth day, Sister Superior, Sister Jude, and Sister Constance came to the parlor with Sister Timothy, who had been in Mrs. McKinstry's class in normal school. The model had been re-enthroned after meticulous dusting, and the plastic pig, stationed at a respectful distance, had been hollowed out to receive a check, for the Sisters believed in preparedness.

Sister Timothy led the conversation adroitly round to the subject which had brought them together. Sister Superior, who was really rather shy, confined her remarks to quiet affirmations of what had just been said. Sister Constance prayed soundlessly that Sister Jude would not disgrace them all.

Mrs. McKinstry was a wizened, white-haired arthritic, who blossomed profusely when cultivated. Since her husband's death, she had experienced a renewal of vigor and, from a complaining semi-invalid, had become a venturesome little grandmother, who drove the car and bought new clothes and went to all the club meetings she had skipped for the last fifteen years. She loved the Sisters, enjoyed reminiscing with them, and asked their prayers for whatever business matters or family problems absorbed her at the moment.

Midway in one of Sister Timothy's most dramatic sentences, Mrs. McKinstry's roving eye fastened on the pig, and she let out a little exclamation of curiosity and delight as she recognized one of the banks from her son's place of business. She would have gone for it immediately, except that Sister Jude anticipated the movement and placed it in her knotted, eager hands. She read the inscription while everyone waited. Everyone, except Sister Constance, who couldn't restrain the remark: "Poetry just seems to go with pigs, don't you think, Mrs. McKinstry?" She lowered her eyes to avoid Sister Jude's swift reproach.

Mrs. McKinstry chuckled and read the rhyme aloud in skittishly pious tones: "A fervent prayer/ An extra penny/ To sanctify many." She reached for her handbag. She rustled about among the lipstick and car keys and Sunday collection envelopes until she found a quarter and three pennies.

"There," she said, bringing them to the surface with a triumphant cluck, "*three* extra pennies and a quarter besides!" She dropped them, one at a time, with a hollow plastic thud, the quarter last, poising it above the slot with a lingering farewell look.

"We knew the Little King would help us," Sister Jude said, interrupting Sister Constance's reflections on the widow's mite. "What a fine *beginning!*" She looked toward Sister Timothy encouragingly.

"Agnes," Sister Timothy said, "wouldn't it be beautiful to have a chapel named for Tom? St. Thomas Chapel . . . There's something so right about it."

Mrs. McKinstry shifted uneasily in her chair. "Of course I'd be thrilled to have you name the chapel for Tom," she said, her voice breaking a little. "Do you intend to build soon?"

"Everything depends upon the necessary funds, Mrs. McKinstry," Sister Jude answered. It was the tone she reserved for bank presidents and auditors from the Bureau of Internal Revenue.

"We were just saying before you came," Sister Timothy said, pressing her advantage, "whoever gives us a major donation—say, anything up to fifty thousand—should have the consolation and the joy of naming the chapel for a dear one."

"I shouldn't think there'd be many folks in Carlton who could give so much," Mrs. McKinstry said. "Where are the African violets you promised to show me?"

Less than two hours later, Sister Constance brought a message to Sister Superior. One of the Franciscan Sisters had called from the hospital to say that Mrs. McKinstry had driven her car into a telephone pole. She was not hurt seriously, just shaken, but in view of her age, the doctor was concerned about the circumstances leading up to the accident. Had they, perhaps, been aware of any emotional disturbance during her visit to the college?

The older members of the community contended that Mrs. McKinstry would come through. Time often worked wonders. Time and prayer. Her brush with death would make her think seriously. Sister Timothy announced that she was putting the whole matter in the hands of Agnes's Guardian Angel, and her evening vigils in the chapel lengthened visibly.

Father Morgan's years in the movie capital had given him a theatrical air. He had mastered the gestures: the flow of the hands, wrists leading like a ballet dancer, and the three-quarter profile with compelling eyes. But Sister Constance felt that the parish public address system and his own vibrato reduced Father Morgan's Hooper Rating when it came to delivery. The more emphatic portions of his Sunday sermons rattled the chandeliers in the high-ceilinged sanctuary, making her yearn for the dramatic pause and the whispered resonance that signaled his Master's voice.

His eloquence had been instrumental in building the new church, it was true, and he was in general favor among the parishioners, especially the women. But even the men appeared to derive vicarious enjoyment from his preaching, sitting with folded arms and eyes rolled upwards to the towering pulpit.

Today he was launching a drive for the parish hall. Some of the old-timers said that it wasn't really needed, but others accused them of obstructing progress. St. Clement's was a growing parish with an up-to-date school, a well-planned, well-built rectory (the old one had been converted to a convent for the Sisters who taught the parish school), and plans for an eighty-five-thousand-dollar hall, complete with stainless steel automatic kitchen, auditorium, meeting rooms, recreation area, nursery facilities, and baby sitters for children whose parents were attending church services.

While Father Morgan outlined the need, Sister Constance trimmed the budget by thirty thousand. That would be a good beginning for their chapel, she thought. Get that close to the goal, and everyone would tax his ingenuity to do more. But of course it was out of the question. As an institution owned and operated by the teaching Congregation to which she belonged (or more accurately, by the loan company which had financed the building), the college was not entitled to Church support.

Father Morgan had reached the part about needing the co-operation of "every man, woman, and child in this parish if we are to succeed in this gigantic undertaking for the glory of God." Sister Constance looked at him and wished that he would reserve his hypnotic powers for more willing victims.

After Mass Father Morgan took the children's envelopes to the convent so that the Sisters could count the money. On his way he passed by the college and stopped to ask the superior's help in reaching the college students of this parish.

Sister Constance greeted him at the door, led him into the reception room, and went in quest of Sister Superior. She returned and found Father Morgan thoughtfully examining the plastic pig.

Nobody knew exactly what happened, but soon afterwards, the piggy banks were gathered up again and stored away in the bursar's cupboard—all except one, which had slipped out of sight behind a row of books in Sister Superior's office. Sister Constance used to see it there when she dusted the furniture in the morning, and it gave her a gloomy satisfaction to know that the animal was at large. Much as she had hated the bald beggary and the doggerel, she hated pettiness more, and on good days she constructed fierce fantasies in which the wandering pig disgorged five-figure bank notes with "Sisters' Chapel" franked into the grain.

May was unusually warm that year, and Sister Constance found the hour and one-half required for morning prayer, meditation, and Mass longer than she cared to admit. The whir of the electric fan reminded her that it was cooler at the rear of the chapel, but twenty years separated her from the relative comfort in which the senior Sisters sat. Where would she be in twenty years? Still fighting off the drowsiness and the suffocation of this early-morning tryst?

Sister Catherine reached for her rosary, and Sister Constance gathered her skirts closer to keep her neighbor's hand out of a strange pocket. The beads rattled annoyingly, and from somewhere out in the hall, the distracting fragrance of coffee and frying bacon wrestled with her prayer.

She gathered her veil with a practiced twist and brought it forward over her shoulder, edging away from the back of the seat so that Sister Clare might rest her hands on the *prie-dieu*. Fifteen minutes more before Mass. She gathered her distractions into a brief lament and laid them before the tabernacle. Outside, the endless freight cars bumped and shook, invading the chapel with bleating cries and the strong, medicinal odor of sheep dip.

Sister Constance skipped the novena that morning, even though it wasn't Tuesday. She wanted to polish the floor in Sister Superior's office, and it was easier to get started before the Sisters began filing in to ask for bus tokens or advice in dealing with violations of dormitory regulations.

The janitor stuck his head in the doorway. "Do you want some more wax to keep the shine on?" He held the mop carefully away from his freshly laundered overalls.

He applied the wax with eager scrupulosity, for in his eighteen years at the college, Otto had contracted some of the Sisters' passion for perfection. He moved the chairs gently aside, sought out the corners, avoiding the baseboards, and gave the space beneath the radiator two coats.

"By golly," he said, frowning at the black marks around the desk, "we got to take all the wax off and clean it before summer school. You tell me when. Maybe Sister Superior go away." He picked up the plastic pig, shook it, and held it out to Sister Constance.

"This pig sounds empty," he said. He backed out gingerly, waiting for the wax to dry. "I put three dimes in the one in the hall before they take it away. You got enough?"

Sister Constance looked ruefully at the wet wax and stuffed the bank in her pocket. She gave him a quick lesson in elementary economics, carefully omitting Father Morgan's part in the total scheme. Otto is so good, she thought. We take vows of poverty and obedience, and he keeps them. She unwound the cord and plugged the polisher into the wall outlet.

"Say," Otto said excitedly, forgetting to tiptoe in his eagerness, "maybe we get the chapel anyway?" He reached into his pocket, pulled out his billfold, and extracted two small pieces of paper. "Sweepstakes tickets," he said. "Maybe we win fifty thousand *pounds*. You know how much a pound is? That be enough?"

"These tickets cost between three and four dollars," Sister Jude said evenly, as Sister Constance, following Sister Superior's orders, left them in the bursar's office. "And he's bought two of them. Why didn't he give the *money* to the chapel instead?"

"There's really only ticket," Sister Constance said. "The other is a confirmation. Be sure to put them away carefully. Otto says you have to produce the ticket if you win. He almost lost a thousand dollars once because he forgot where he put the thing."

The Community was split on the Sweepstakes Question, and for once the division was not chronological. Sister Timothy, the oldest in the house, was not one to condone gambling, but she was a firm believer in charity. Didn't the tickets say plainly that this was a hospital benefit? It was really another form of the corporal works of mercy, you know, and the Irish sense of compassion is much stronger than anything we find here in America.

Sister Timothy wanted to put the tickets beneath the Infant's statue in the chapel. Or maybe St. Joseph's because it was larger, but Sister Superior objected on the grounds that it savored of superstition and seemed like putting limits on God's power.

Sister Constance, tempted by the ironic possibilities of the situation, succumbed. The notion of building a chapel

on sweepstakes winnings was so delightfully incongruous
that it blurred her judgment for a time. The strangeness
that others attribute to fate she identified with Divine
Providence, and she told herself that it would be just like
God to answer their prayers in this unexpected fashion.

But she knew she was dramatizing. In certain characters
there is an intermittent romance between cynicism and
naïveté, and Sister Constance was one of these. So it didn't
surprise her when June 6 came and went without a tele-
gram of victory. Sister Timothy took the silence harder,
and padded about the house with pinched features, pulling
the black shawl closer about her shoulders, and saying at
intervals, "I don't understand it. God must have some
magnificent treat in store for us."

The community bell rang at four-thirty the next afternoon,
and since it was neither the day for Confessions nor for
Holy Hour, the Sisters were all asking the reason for the
summons. They stood about in the community room keeping a token silence, impatient to be about their work but
too obedient to ignore the bell. Sister Superior and Sister
Jude entered together, their faces serious, their eyes taking
a quick census before the business began.

At Sister Superior's direction, the Sisters seated themselves after a brief offering and waited with folded arms,
their hands concealed within the large outer sleeves.

"Sister Jude has something to tell us about the chapel,"
Sister Superior said, and the community searched her face
for an answer to their prayers but found no clue.

Sister Jude glanced at Sister Superior. "We've really
been very fortunate," she began.

"I knew it!" Sister Timothy said. "I knew something
would come of all those prayers," but Sister Jude looked

sharply at her, and Sister Superior nodded to Sister Jude to go on.

"As you know, the fire department has inspected our building," Sister Jude said, "and *they* feel that our chapel is . . . inadequate." The Sisters began talking all at once, and Sister Superior tapped her ring for silence. Sister Jude hurried toward the climax.

"We have to put in another exit," she said. "The aisles are so narrow—and an outside stairway." She took an envelope from her pocket. "This is the official notice."

"Providentially," Sister Jude said, "we have the money to do what is required." She looked with deference toward the head table and said, "Maybe Sister Superior would like to tell you about the changes in schedule before I presént the financial part."

"For a while, at least," Sister Superior said, "we'll have to have two Masses. The younger Sisters up to and including Sister Constance will rise half an hour earlier—at five instead of five-thirty." She smiled to cushion the shock. "The workmen would like to start at eight each morning, so please try to get your private devotions in before that time or after five P.M. Our noon examination of conscience will be in the community room." She turned the meeting back to Sister Jude, now thoroughly in command of the situation, and ready for a detailed report in which the light of her business acumen gleamed from a bushel of extraneous data. The estimated cost of the remodeling was three hundred dollars. Two of the windows would have to be sealed off, but on good days they could have the fire door open. They couldn't afford to have the whole interior refinished, so it might not be beautiful to look at, but then the chapel was only temporary anyway.

Sister Timothy began asking the Sister nearest her to repeat what Sister Superior had said. "It's awful to get old," she complained. "It sounded to me as if Sister Superior said we'd get up at five."

Sister Constance turned unwillingly as Sister Jude spoke again. "One more thing, Sisters," she said. "Sister Superior and I have been talking this over, and we've agreed that is is a blessing in disguise. If we hadn't had the banks, of course, there would be no provision for meeting this added burden."

If we hadn't had the banks, Sister Constance thought, there would be no burden. But she merely meant that it would have been a different one.

"Perhaps you know," Sister Jude said, "our chapel fund was a little more than three hundred and sixty dollars, and Sister Superior has a wonderful idea for the other sixty dollars. Sister Superior blinked when the gentle rod of her authority coiled in Sister Jude's aggressive hand.

Sister Jude seemed not to notice. "We were down at Jamison's today," she said, her voice growing slightly nasal, "and we found a perfectly lovely statue of the Infant of Prague." She smiled expectantly and looked around.

Sister Constance averted her eyes. Already she realized that the odds favored 100 per cent attendance at tomorrow's novena. It didn't really matter when or how they got the chapel. What mattered was that they kept on wanting one. She smiled with what Sister Jude was sure to interpret as satisfaction over the new statue. Then she plunged a hand deep into her pocket and loosened the sticky rhyme that still clung to the plastic pig.

MOTHER COAKLEY'S REFORM
by Brendan Gill

Even in old age, Mother Coakley was as round and smooth-skinned as a ripe chestnut. In her billowing black habit, she had always the air of being about to be caught up in a gust of mountain wind and carried aloft to the sunny, well-scrubbed corner awaiting her in heaven. Despite the mother superior's hints of disapproval, hints which by anyone else would have been taken as commands, Mother Coakley enjoyed playing tennis with the younger convent girls. The tennis court was on the crest of a hill behind the ramshackle wooden buildings which made up the convent chapel and school; and what seemed in the North Carolina town below an agreeable summer breeze approached—on that dusty oblong of root-ribbed and rocky court—the force and temperature of a winter's gale. Luckily, Mother Coakley paid no attention to temperatures, hot or cold. Gathering the full skirts of her habit into her left hand, she scampered about the court like an energetic chipmunk, letting her veil float out behind her in ghostly disarray, and only just showing the tops of her high black shoes. She had learned to play tennis as a novice at the mother house in France, no one knew how many years ago, and she played it unexpectedly well. Like most people who learned the game in the nineteenth century, she felt no real interest in volleying. She was willing to lose point after point in order to attempt a smashing forehand drive, or to drop an occasional cut shot over the net; and when she had succeeded in doing so, the ball being unreturnable, Mother Coakley would drop her racquet and clap her hands in unaffected delight.

She had no use, in fact, for any of the effete mannerisms
of latter-day tennis. If she failed to return an opponent's
serve, she never called, "Good shot," but, screwing up her
face into an expression of self-contempt, would announce
sharply, "I should have had it! I should have had it!" As
she played, her cheeks grew more and more deeply suffused with blood. Though she looked as if she might be
about to suffer a stroke, she never heeded suggestions that
it would be sensible to rest for a few minutes between sets.
"I always get to look like this," she would say, panting
heartily. The French neatness of speech taught her at the
mother house in Dijon would then slur away to a soft Irish
brogue. "Sure, I got to look like this when I was six."
Also, as she continued to play, her rosary, carelessly
stuffed inside her heavy black belt, would work itself loose
and flail about her waist until finally, with tears of excitement streaming down her cheeks and wisps of clipped gray
hair showing at the sides of her wimple, she would be
forced to stop playing. "If I didn't stop now, I'd strangle
myself on my own beads," she would say. "But for them,
I'd be playing till dark."

She usually contrived, however, to retire from the game
while she was still winning. This mild vanity was one of the
two or three enormous sins with which she wrestled all but
visibly from year to year. It was noted by the other nuns in
the convent that Mother Coakley spent more than twice as
much time in the confessional during the height of the tennis season as she did during the rest of the year. They never
commented on this directly, but sometimes they would
tease her, out of love and curiosity, as she left the chapel.
"Goodness, you took a long time saying your penance,"
they would whisper, climbing the steep, worn stairs to their

cells. "Father Nailer must have been in a dreadful temper
by the time you reached him." Mother Coakley, who, after Mother Bonnet, was the oldest nun in age and point of
service in the convent, would flush and answer, in a pretext
of anger, "*Attendez!* What kind of talk is that? *Vous savez
les règles!*"

Mother Bonnet preferred to remain at the convent, except when, as mother superior, she had official business to
transact, and it was Mother Coakley's duty and joy to
shepherd the girls of the school on their occasional visits to
town. She was well acquainted in all the shops around the
square. She helped the girls to choose gloves and girdles,
and chaste perfumes, which she always referred to as
"toilet water." The mother superior frowned on the use of
perfumes and girdles, but Mother Coakley answered her
objections by saying mildly, "God love them, we'll be
lucky if that's all the harm they do with their money."
During every such visit to town it was customary to drop in
at Mr. Feinman's little combination cigar and sports shop
on the square and pick up tennis or ping-pong balls, and to
cap the afternoon by drinking chocolate frosteds at Fater's
corner drugstore. Mother Coakley never ate or drank anything while in town, but she liked to purchase from Mrs.
Fater, as unobtrusively as possible, a ten-cent Hershey bar,
which she would slip into one of her capacious interior
pockets. "Energy food," she would say, making her eyes
round and bright. "When you get to be my age . . ."

Mother Coakley's age was one of the few secrets which
she had been able to carry over from her girlhood outside
the convent, but she must have been past seventy when the
mother superior attempted to take a stand on the subject
of her playing tennis. Mother Bonnet, who was as lean and

slow moving as Mother Coakley was plump and bouncing, had never approved of the latter's athletic activities, and as the years went by it seemed to her less and less appropriate for one of Mother Coakley's age and position to be making of herself, as mother superior said, "a gross spectacle truly." She had been looking for an excuse to put an end to the display and the incident in Mr. Feinman's shop was more than enough, she felt, to justify speaking soberly to her.

One winter day, while Mother Bonnet was engaged in her annual skirmish with the tax collector in his office beside the courthouse, Mother Coakley and five or six of the girls spent a strenuous two hours shopping and walking about the town. The girls bought writing paper, cotton stockings, and some sensible, oversize sweaters, and enjoyed the usual chocolate frosteds at Fater's while Mother Coakley bought, and concealed on her person, the usual ten-cent Hershey bar. Having a few minutes to spare before rejoining Mother Bonnet, they decided to stop off at Mr. Feinman's. Though it was February, the midday sun was always bright and the tennis court was in no worse condition than it would be in June; Mother Coakley and the girls played nearly every afternoon, glorying in their indifference to the calendar. One of the girls had been planning for some time to buy a new racquet, but Mother Coakley and Mr. Feinman had yet to come to terms.

Today, welcoming them, Mr. Feinman swore that he had just what the doctor ordered. He brought out from the dusty shelves at the back of the store, where he kept piled in indiscriminate confusion cases of cigars and baseball mitts, a racquet called the Bluebird Special. "Sweetest little racquet I ever had in the place," Mr. Feinman said, blowing off the dust and hefting the racquet with professional care. Mr. Feinman had never played any game more taxing than pinochle, but he knew how to sell merchandise. He stroked the gut with his fingers. "Like music," he said. "With this racquet is easy wictory. Is steady wictory."

Mother Coakley enjoyed shopping. She particularly enjoyed haggling with her old friend Mr. Feinman. The girls formed an interested half circle about her as she took up the challenge, and a few of the inevitable courthouse loungers gathered at the open door of the shop. Mother Coakley swept this familiar audience with a glance, then, turning to Mr. Feinman, she asked simply, "How much?"

Mr. Feinman held up his hands as if to ward off the wounding mention of money. "For such a racquet? For workmanship like this?"

"How much?" Mother Coakley repeated.

Mr. Feinman consented, with a shrug, to discuss the sordid question. "Ten dollars."

Mother Coakley tapped her broad black belt, making the wooden rosary beads rattle as if in reproach. "Nonsense," she said. When she bargained, she seemed purely French; even her voice took on the accents of Dijon in place of those of Dublin. "It isn't worth five."

Mr. Feinman appealed to the girls behind Mother Coakley and, by extension, to the crowd outside the door. "Five dollars! A work of art for five dollars!" He raised his eyes to the stamped tin ceiling over his head. "May God strike me dead if I didn't pay six dollars for it wholesale. I can—"

"Leave God out of this," Mother Coakley interrupted promptly. "What kind of pagan chatter is that?" She took the racquet from Mr. Feinman's hands and began to execute a few tentative strokes, cutting at and lobbing an imaginary ball. What happened next no one was able after-

ward to decide. Some people thought that Mr. Feinman
had caught sight of the mother superior nearing the entrance to his store and had leaned forward to welcome her.
Others thought that he had detected a price tag dangling
from the end of the racquet and, being uncertain of what it
said, had bent down to retrieve it. In any event, he lowered
his head in time to receive, on his left temple, the full force
of one of Mother Coakley's savage forehand drives. He
dropped in his tracks like a sack of meal, without so much
as a moan.

The girl who had intended to buy the racquet began to
cry hysterically, "He did it! God did it! God did it!"
Mother Coakley knelt beside the motionless figure of Mr.
Feinman, her round cheeks looking oddly drawn and pale.
"He's not dead," she said sharply, "he can't be. He's
breathing. You can see he's breathing." She drew the Hershey bar from her pocket and, breaking off a piece, attempted to force it between Mr. Feinman's lips. At that
moment he opened his eyes. In another moment he was on
his knees. Slowly, painfully, he pulled himself up. "Is
nothing," he said faintly. "Is just a tap."

Mother Coakley had barely begun her apology when another, deeper voice reached her over the heads of the
crowd. "*Tais-toi,*" said the mother superior. "I am in
charge here." She worked her way through the crowd, her
habit rustling with authority. She stared first at Mr. Feinman, half crumpled against the counter, and then at
Mother Coakley, still armed with the Bluebird Special.
"The racquet," she said to Mr. Feinman. "One of the girls
is buying this racquet?"

Mr. Feinman nodded.

"How much?"

With the air of a man who knows that it is useless to fight against the power of God, Mr. Feinman said brokenly, "Seven fifty. For a work of art, I will take seven fifty."

The mother superior, fresh from her annual triumph over the tax collector, said, "Very well." She set seven dollars and fifty cents on the counter. Then, turning to the girls, she made a gesture with her hands like that of a farmer's wife scattering hens. "Now, then, *dépêchons.*"

The little group was halfway across the square before the mother superior spoke to Mother Coakley. "You and your wretched tennis!" she said bluntly.

Mother Coakley nodded. "I have been thinking it over. I have come to feel that perhaps you are right." She pursed her lips. "Perhaps I am getting old."

"I have wanted you to make your own decision," said the mother superior. She was always glad to be able to temper sternness with magnanimity. Besides, she and Mother Coakley were old friends, and it would be cruel to make her humble herself too far. "It is not that I am angry about this merely. Accidents can happen to anybody."

"No, it was my fault," Mother Coakley said, her voice softening to the brogue. She slipped a piece of the Hershey bar into her mouth. "I shall have to give up my forehand drive. You were right in thinking that I should have done so long ago." Then, despite her best efforts at self-control, her feet began to skip along the asphalt sidewalk. "From now on," she said penitently, "I shall play as badly as I can."

THE SONG AT THE SCAFFOLD
by Gertrud von Le Fort

CHAPTER I

Paris, October 1794.

In your letter to me, my dear friend, you emphasize the extraordinarily brave attitude with which women, the so-called weaker sex, face death every day of these terrible times. And you are right. With admiration you cite the pose of "noble" Madame Roland, of "queenly" Marie-Antoinette, of "wonderful" Charlotte Corday and "heroic" Mademoiselle de Sombreuil. (I am quoting your own adjectives.) You conclude with the touching sacrifice of the sixteen Carmelite nuns of Compiègne who mounted the guillotine singing *Veni Creator;* and you also mention the poignant and steadfast voice of young Blanche de la Force who finished the hymn that the executioner's knife silenced on the lips of her companions. "How nobly," you say toward the end of your eloquent letter, "the dignity of man triumphs in all these martyrs of the kingdom, of the Gironde and of the persecuted Church, martyrs caught in the waves of devastating chaos."

O dear disciple of Rousseau! As always I admire your cheerful and noble faith in the indestructible nobility of human nature even when mankind is tasting most desolate failure. But chaos is nature too, my friend, the executioner of your women martyrs, the beast in man, fear and terror —all these are nature too! Since I am far closer to the frightful happenings in Paris than you, who have emigrated, permit me to confess candidly that I interpret the amazing resignation of those who die every day less as an

inherent natural grace than as the last supreme effort of a
vanishing culture. Ah, yes! you despise culture, my dear
friend, but we have learned to appreciate its value again, to
respect conventional forms which prescribe restraint even
to mortal terror and—in a few cases—something quite different.

Blanche de la Force was the last on your list of heroines.
And yet she was not a heroine in your sense of the word.
She was not elected to demonstrate the nobility of mankind but rather to prove the infinite frailty of all our
vaunted powers. Sister Marie de l'Incarnation, the only
surviving nun of Compiègne, confirmed me in this idea.

But perhaps you do not even know that Blanche de la
Force was a former nun of Compiègne? She was a novice
there for a considerable period of time. Let me tell you a
little of this exceedingly important episode of her life! For I
believe it is the beginning of the famous song at the foot of
the scaffold.

You know the Marquis de la Force, Blanche's father. So
I need not tell you of his esteem for the skeptical writings
of Voltaire and Diderot. You have heard of his sympathy
for certain liberal patriots of the Palais Royal. His trends
were purely theoretical and he never dreamed of concrete
results. This sophisticated aristocrat did not think that the
subtle spice of his conversation would ever season the
crude cookery of the people. But let us not criticize the sad
errors of our poor friend, for he, like so many others, has
atoned for them. (Ah! my friend, when all is said and
done, most of us were very like him.) Here we are only
concerned with the motive that could induce a man like the
Marquis de la Force to entrust his daughter to a convent.

While Blanche was in Compiègne, I spoke to her father
on a few occasions in the cafés of the Palais Royal where

he was rhapsodizing about liberty and fraternity with similarly minded friends. Whenever anyone asked him about his daughter he answered ruefully that he considered "the prisons of religion"—this was his name for convents—as undesirable as those of the state. Nevertheless he was forced to admit that his daughter felt happy there, happy and safe. "Poor timid child," he usually added, "the sad circumstances of her birth apparently determined her whole attitude toward life." And this, indeed, was the common view of the matter.

You, my dear friend, will scarcely understand the Marquis' allusion, because at the time he has reference to, you yourself were still a child. He was speaking of the notorious fire-works catastrophe at the wedding of Louis the Sixteenth, then a dauphin, with the daughter of the emperor of Austria.

Later this catastrophe was regarded as an evil omen that foreshadowed the fate of the royal pair. Well, perhaps it was not merely an omen but also a symbol of fate. (For revolutions are caused and conditioned, to be sure, by mismanagement and mistakes in the existing system. But their essential character is the violent outbreak of the deadly fear of an epoch approaching its end. And it is this I had in mind when I spoke of a symbol.)

For it is not at all true that neglect on the part of the authorities was responsible for the unfortunate accident on the square of Louis the Fifteenth. This rumor was spread by people who wished to delude themselves about the mystery of that sudden and violent error of the masses. Mystery, as you know, is intolerably annoying to enlightenment such as ours! As a matter of fact, the authorities were at their post. All the usual precautions had been taken with model efficiency. The carriages of the nobility, and among them the conveyance of the young Marquise de la Force, who was an expectant mother, were greeted respectfully by the crowd of pedestrians near the heavy water wagons of the *pompiers,* which were conscientiously held in readiness for all emergencies. Police officers stood at the intersections of the streets which ran into the square, and kept order. In spite of the "wretched times," which were almost proverbial, people looked well-dressed and well-fed. Practically every individual represented a well-to-do burgher of decent thinking and behavior. It was difficult to imagine them as part of the anarchistic chaos of half an hour later. For they were full of eager anticipation of a festive spectacle and responded to the police in orderly fashion. In short, the dreadful incident which followed was sudden and inexplicable. For it was an omen.

A harmless little blaze in the room where the fireworks were stored, and wild and instant panic, although there was absolutely no danger, caused mad confusion. At the street corner the policemen were unable to make a gesture—for they had disappeared! The happy and loyal citizens had disappeared. There remained only a wild monster, a mass of human beings stifled by their own terror: it was chaos that slumbers in the depths of all things and breaks through the solid armor of habit and custom.

Through the windows of her fine carriage, in the midst of that fearful throng, the Marquise saw a gruesome spectacle. She heard the despairing cries of those who had fallen to the ground, she heard the groans of trodden bodies. But she herself was as safe in her great coach as if she had been on a ship secure on storm-tossed seas. Involuntarily she put out her slender, aristocratic hand and bolted the door. The bolt was a little rusty because the coach hailed from the time of the Fronde, when all carriage doors had been supplied with bolts since one never knew when there might be occasion for flight. But these bolts had not been used for a long time! The Marquise felt quite safe though she was considerably disturbed! This is not surprising for the sight of a crowd is always painful to the individual. Now whether the horses, confused by the noise and the turmoil, began to run of themselves, or whether the coachman lost his head and tried to escape, at any rate the coach began to move and drove straight into the screaming, raging, despairing crowd. Almost at once the horses were stopped and the carriage door forced open. Seething chaos followed. For a moment there was something that resembled the revolution to come.

"Madame!" shrieked a man who bore a blood-stained child in his arms, "you are safe and secure in your coach while the people are dying under the hooves of your horses! But soon, I tell you, it is you who will be dying and we shall sit in your coaches." And even as he spoke the Marquise saw his menacing expression mirrored in hundreds of terror-stricken faces. In another moment she had been dragged from her carriage and her own expression of fear merged with that of the mass.

Rumor had it later that Blanche de la Force was born in the half-wrecked carriage on the way home from the square. This is an exaggeration. But it is true that the Marquise arrived at her palace on foot with torn garments and the face of a Medusa, and that, as the result of her terrible experience, she was confined prematurely and died soon afterwards.

Now I do not hesitate to associate the temperament of the poor child with the circumstances of her birth. Not only the superstition of the people but the opinion of qualified physicians consider such a connection quite possible.

Blanche, thrust into the world too soon through the fright
of her mother, seemed to have been dowered only with
fear. At an early age she displayed a timidity which greatly
exceeded the little fears one usually observes in children.
(Children are afraid of all sorts of things and one is apt to
consider this a lack of understanding.) If her own little dog
barked suddenly, she trembled; and she recoiled from the
face of a new servant as though he were a ghost. It was impossible to cure her of fearing a niche in the passage which
she passed every day with her nurse. At the sight of a dead
bird or snail in the garden she froze to a statue. It seemed
as if this pathetic little person lived in constant expectation
of some shocking event which she might perhaps avoid by
eternal watchfulness like that of small sick creatures who
sleep with open eyes; or as if the great fear in her childish
gaze penetrated the firm exterior of a sheltered life to a
core of terrible frailty.

"Are you sure the stairs will not slip from under my
feet?" she inquired when she was taken to the solid tower
of the Château la Force, the ancestral home of her race,
where the Marquis spent the summer. This tower had already defied seven centuries and everyone could see that it
was capable of lasting seven more. "Won't the wall tip
over? Are you sure the gondola will not sink? Won't people get angry?" This was the kind of thing little Blanche
was constantly asking. And there was no use explaining to
her that there was no cause for alarm. She would listen at-
tentively and reflect on everything she was told, for she
was by no means unintelligent, but she continued to be
afraid. Neither affection nor severity nor her own in-
dubitable willingness to improve, altered her unfortunate
temperament. Indeed her very willingness made matters

worse for she became so depressed by the futility of her efforts that she considered the lack of that courage which everyone urged upon her as the most shameful disgrace. One might almost say that in addition to everything else she grew to be afraid of her own fear. I have said that Blanche was not unintelligent; she had a good mind and so in time she invented little devices to mask the true state of affairs. She no longer asked: "Won't the stairs slip from under me?" or, "Are you sure the gondola will not sink?" But she would suddenly feel tired or ill, she had forgotten to learn her lesson or to fetch something she needed. In short there was some reason or other why she could not set foot on the stairs or in the gondola.

The servants laughed and dubbed her "rabbit-heart" but she did not improve, she even suffered more than formerly from her weakness because now she was trying to hide it. Sometimes one could see the agonies she was enduring. Never before had there been a comely child of noble birth who moved with such awkward timidity, who blushed so unfortunately as Blanche de la Force. The great title of her family was like a placard she bore unrightfully; the proud name of de la Force was idle mockery. No one who remembered her little face that paled so easily could call her anything but just Blanche. But "rabbit" was after all the most suitable name of all. This was the state of affairs when the Marquis de la Force engaged Madame de Chalais.

This excellent governess undertook Blanche's religious instruction with decision and thoroughness and by this approach succeeded in overcoming the child's fears to a certain extent. For because of the liberal tendencies of the Marquis, this aspect of her education had been deplorably neglected up to this time, and since Blanche, unlike her father, had the pronounced needs of a religious nature, the omission must have been especially fatal for her.

From a psychological point of view Madame de Chalais was probably wise in directing her young pupil's attention to the Christ Child before everything else. It was Blanche's first encounter with *"le petit Roi de Gloire."* (You, my dear friend, are acquainted with this charming little wax figure of the Carmelite convent in Compiègne, a figure that delighted the children at Christmas time when it was exhibited in the chapel.)

Le petit Roi had a crown and a scepter of gold which the King of France had given Him to show that *le petit Roi* was the ruler of heaven and earth. In gratitude for his gift, *le petit Roi* protected the King and his people: and so it was quite possible to live safely in France without having to think of slipping stairs and tottering walls. Only, of course, one must give due reverence to *le petit Roi,* just as the King always did. One could do this without bestowing crowns and scepters, by prayers and little acts of love, obedience and worship. If one was conscientious in all these things one might depend upon the protection of *le petit Roi* as confidently as the King of France himself. Well, I have told you that Blanche had a religious nature and yet in the beginning Madame de Chalais met with unexpected obstacles. In later years she preferred to keep silence on that score, although as a rule she liked to indulge in reminiscences of her educational methods.

"Surely you must see how easy it is for the King of Heaven to protect you," she once said to Blanche in her gentle obstinate way when the child was again hesitating to go upstairs. "Only think of the great power of even our own king on earth!"

Blanche lifted her troubled little face to her governess. Sometimes her tremulous glances resembled flocks of restless birds. "But if He lost His crown?" she asked pensively.

For a moment Madame de Chalais was nonplussed. It was true that this objection had never occurred to her. But almost instantly she rejected it—she was very apt in rejecting uncomfortable questions. Blanche sometimes imagined that they rebounded from the whalebones of her bodice which was a little too tight for her.

"You cannot believe in all seriousness, Blanche," she said, "that one loses one's crown as easily as a handkerchief. But one must have the proper respect for it! You promised me never to omit your prayer, and so you may rest assured that the King of Heaven will never fail to protect you. You can really go up the stairs without worrying."

Blanche quailed. It was the very stairway about which she had always asked whether it would slip from her. Involuntarily she freed her hand from the clasp of her governess and groped for one of the supports of the banister. And Fate had it that the support broke!

The little frightened birds in Blanche's eyes fluttered to Madame de Chalais in terror. For a moment fear and security regarded each other almost with hostility. Then it suddenly seemed as if not the stairs but Madame de Chalais slipped, as though she had assumed the rôle of the child.

"How can you frighten me so?" she cried. And she recoiled a little so that the bones of her tight bodice crackled softly.

Of course this mood did not last long. Madame de Chalais was not accustomed to yield to moods. And, as I have

already said, Blanche's resistance weakened at that time
when the ideas and symbols of Christian piety were crowding out the uncertain phantasies of fear from her imagination. I can quite understand this. Ah, my friend, what
consolation there is in faith! From my own childhood days
I remember the strange penetration of prayer through all
the layers of being down to the very foundation of all
things where falling is possible no longer. Undoubtedly
Blanche must have had similar sensations. The poor child
who had stubbornly refused all earthly guaranties of safety
began to confide her little anxious heart to the shelter of
the Supreme Power. The little rabbit took courage. Madame de Chalais even had the satisfaction of seeing her
smile at her own former fears and of mocking them in mischievous jests that savored a little of youthful boasting but
satisfied everyone nevertheless.

She was sixteen now, slender, with a small delicate
mouth and a face that looked a little peaked and strained.
Madame de Chalais had been careful to accustom her to a
bodice as tight as her own, and so the girl's movements
were graceful but somewhat constrained. No one, however, would have called her shy. Since everything had
turned out so favorably, the Marquis de la Force set about
planning a suitable marriage for his daughter. But Madame de Chalais surprised him with the information that
Blanche did not wish to marry, but that she desired to become a nun.

CHAPTER II

Now you can easily imagine that a man like the Marquis de la Force, who agreed with the most brilliant intellects in France that the Church was an institution of the past, raised objections. His friends heard him remark in high ill-humor that he had set his hopes upon Madame de Chalais and that all she had done after all was to build for Blanche a bridge by which the child could conveniently quit this world. She was just as fearful as ever, most likely! And the Marquis reasoned that for certain natures the vast confusion of life ends in the convent where definite boundaries are set to the welter of possibilities, where Destiny offers no unanticipated challenge or violence, where life moves amid firm-fixed regulations and thoughts and walls. And the latter, so the Marquis expressed himself, did not open upon reality but only to the pleasant illusion of Heaven and its inhabitants.

Now although his train of thought was certainly distorted, he was faintly right as far as Blanche's decision was concerned. But it would have been most unjust to the young girl to weigh only such considerations! We must repeat again and again that Blanche was really religious. In Carmel de Compiègne, where Madame de Chalais had connections, she made the very best impression. When she was introduced to the Prioress—at that time the invalid Prioress Croissy was still living—she answered the question as to whether she did not fear the severe regulations of the convent with the tinge of boastfulness she now displayed in matters of courage: "Oh, Reverend Mother, truly there are other things to be feared more than these slight sacrifices!"

Thereupon the Prioress (whom Madame de Chalais had told of Blanche's former difficulties) took occasion to ask her of what, for instance, she would be afraid.

Blanche reflected for a moment. Then she answered less positively than at first:

"I do not know, Holy Mother, but if you bid me, I shall think about it and answer you later."

"I do not bid you," Madame de Croissy replied quickly. She was still young at that time but already marked by the wasting disease of which she died soon after. They say that God put upon her a great dread of death some time before she died (it was then that she prayed so often in the convent garden and that therefore she felt sympathy for Blanche). As a matter of fact it is not altogether usual that a religious order as severe as that of the Carmelites should have admitted so frail a young girl.

So Blanche de la Force entered upon her enclosure and we are told that her strained little face shone with such fervent happiness that everyone in Carmel de Compiègne was convinced of her vocation and believed that she would become a worthy daughter of Saint Teresa.

She was a satisfactory postulant. It was not altogether easy for her to observe the strict regulations of the order— still she observed them. She was amiable, eager, obedient, and—this must be emphasized particularly—she was happy and grateful too. This was especially pronounced when disquieting rumors crossed the threshold of the convent. And that was hardly avoidable in those times. (It was shortly before the summoning of the Estates General.) We are told that on such occasions Blanche's expression was one of indescribable contentment, that she even clapped her hands childishly and exclaimed with a trace of gay arrogance, "That does not concern us here." Or, "It won't reach us! We are safe here."

Just as she had once repeated the easy maxims of Madame de Chalais, so now she adopted certain heroic locutions in the style of the Carmelites, "O God, to Thee do I sacrifice myself completely!" Or, "O Suffering, sweet peace to the lovers of God, many I learn to know thee!" But gradually the words she had learned to repeat so effortlessly had their effect upon her—and certain reactions took place.

This became particularly evident when, at about this time, the Prioress Croissy died. Her death struggle was very painful. For hours the sound of her moaning filled the convent. Blanche was bewildered and shocked and asked how it was possible that God permitted so holy a woman to suffer so. She exhibited such horror and apprehension that the whole convent was amazed. Indeed, her investiture was postponed at the time because Sister Marie de l'Incarnation, the novice mistress, was seized with doubt. But in the end it took place quite suddenly.

It was the year seventeen hundred and eighty-nine and the national assembly convening at Versailles was taking action against church property as a relief measure for the financial depression of the country. (You will probably recall the decision I have in mind.)

Already that summer the superior of the Carmelite Order, Monsignore Rigaud, had informed the convents under his jurisdiction that a law which forbade the admission of new members was pending. Monsignore did not hesitate to disclose that the national assembly was contemplating the complete suppression of religious orders. But there was hope, he said, that the law might be altered to permit those who were already members to remain so, and to allow them to die out. In consideration of these circumstances Monsignore advised the immediate investiture of postulants unless there were some special individual objection. This wise and liberal prelate wrote: "Let us confide these young girls to the guidance of God unless there are unambiguous reasons against such a procedure, and let us not be petty but liberal in regard to them. For in time to come, God himself will choose and distinguish between them. "Christ," so the letter concluded, "may be said to be in the garden of Gethsemane. I therefore recommend the name of Jésus au Jardin de l'Agonie for the postulants since under the conditions prevailing today no more suitable name could be found." (You know, my friend, that in Carmelite convents they believe that the religious name the individual Sister receives at her investiture gives her special access to the mystery expressed by that name.)

Under these circumstances the newly elected prioress, Madame Lidoine (her religious name was Sister Theresa of Saint Augustin), thought it advisable to confer about Blanche with the novice mistress, Sister Marie de l'Incarnation.

But let us learn the upshot of this discussion from Sister Marie de l'Incarnation herself or, as the children of the charming singer Rose Ducor called her, Sister Marie of the Christchild, for that is how their mother had explained the unintelligible name of de l'Incarnation to them.

You know, my friend, how this singer surprised us in the days of the revolution! In the world of the theater she was a veritable little goddess and some of her more frivolous

admirers had accused her of coquetting with religion. But
during the Reign of Terror she sheltered various priests
and members of religious orders in her own home protected by her immense popularity. (Ah, my dear friend,
people frequently surprise us by their steadfastness in the
face of martyrdom. I shall never dare to express any
positive views on these matters.) For a time Marie de l'Incarnation enjoyed the hospitality of Rose Ducor and her
escape from the revolutionary tribunal is undoubtedly due
to the calm presence of mind of the little singer.

CHAPTER III

In those days I had the honor of calling on that distinguished nun on several occasions. She was engaged in
writing a biography of her martyred Sisters. I found her
seated at Madam Ducor's graceful desk of rosewood, ar-
ranging all sorts of papers. Of course she wore neither her
robe nor her veil but was dressed in lay clothing, a bonnet
on her head and her kerchief drawn so closely around her
neck that it covered the place where obstinate rumor had
insisted she bore a narrow red scar since the execution of
her Sisters. Even the brave little singer likes to repeat this
touching legend for she considers Marie de l'Incarnation a
saint.

When she noticed that I was looking at her kerchief she
pushed it aside with a sad and tremulous gesture but without a trace of resentment. And I ascertained, as doubt-
lessly she wished me to, that the rumor was false. But I
understood why it had spread. For this woman really had a
most impressive personality. It was easy and natural to believe miracles of her. (When one knows her nothing is
more amazing than the touching name, "Sister Marie of
the Christchild!") She might have served as a model for
the statue of a saintly queen, even of a saintly king. So, at
least, it seemed to me, and I do not think that this feeling
was based only on the knowledge of her origin. You must
know, my friend, that this Sister is supposed to be the natural daughter of a French prince. Up to the time of the

revolution she actually received an income from the state; and it is known that because of her illegitimate birth she required a special dispensation from the bishop to enable her to enter the convent of Carmel. They say that as a young girl she lived in brilliant circumstances and then quite suddenly, at the grave of the Carmelite nun, Madame Acarie, she was seized by a burning desire to expiate the sins of the court (to which she owed her life!), just as Madame Louise de France, the prioress of Carmel de Saint Denis, had done before her. This past history of hers explains a great deal in the life of this rare and noble soul. Well—I stated my question concerning Blanche de la Force.

She gave me a most peculiar answer. It was really another question. "Must fear and horror always be evil? Is it not possible that they may be deeper than courage, something that corresponds far more to the reality of things, to the terrors of the world, and to our own weakness?"

I was greatly astonished at her words for you know, dear friend, that it was Sister Marie de l'Incarnation who persuaded the convent of Carmel de Compiègne to offer Heaven that heroic consecration, which, in a way, foreshadowed the fate of the convent. (I shall speak of that in a moment.)

"So fear is deeper than courage—and you say this, Sister Marie de l'Incarnation?" I asked.

She ignored my allusion to her heroism and went back to my first question.

"As a matter of fact," she said, "there were those among us who approved of Blanche's return to the world. But our Reverend Mother, the Prioress Lidoine of St. Augustin, decided otherwise. Madame Lidoine had the greatest wisdom and knowledge of souls."

"And yet," I replied, "the results have proved that Madame Lidoine was wrong." (I was thinking of Blanche's flight from Compiègne.)

"Not Madame Lidoine," she replied quickly, "but another Sister. For you must know that not all of us understood fully the guidance of our Reverend Mother."

Suddenly I had the unerring though inexplicable conviction that she was speaking of herself. At the same moment she looked at me and I colored under her gaze. She herself remained quite unconcerned.

A brief silence ensued, filled with unspoken thoughts. At last she said, with a strange childlike expression so oddly in contrast with her proud clear-cut features that I was almost confused: "And why should you not know it, Monsieur de Villeroi? Have you not come to learn the truth? I assure you that this truth will glorify His Majesty more than any other!" (For in the convent of Carmel they designate God as His Majesty.)

Then she gave me various documents. Some were notes of the Prioress Lidoine, notes that constituted a sort of journal of her office. And some were written in her own hand, for, as I have already said, she was working at a biography of the martyred Sisters.

I shall draw upon these two manuscripts and relate whatever is of importance to us.

Sister Marie de l'Incarnation urged the Reverend Mother not to permit Blanche's investiture and pointed to her peculiar weakness of fear.

"O Reverend Mother," she said and her beautiful spirited eyes rested upon the Prioress (she could not look up to her since she was considerably taller), "this poor child moves me to compassion for she has sought shelter in the walls of the convent as a bird slips into the nest. I do not love this child less because she is weak. But just because I love her!—O Reverend Mother, the world is so full of little pieties, there are hundreds of these tiny flames! Every day they burn before countless altars of Paris and hosts upon hosts are blown out by the storms of life. Such little flames do not belong in a convent! The Carmelites demand absolute strength and faith!''

Let me interrupt my tale for a moment. I have just described the impression which the personality of Marie de l'Incarnation made upon me, but perhaps I should tell you a little about her position in the convent and above all of her attitude towards the new prioress.

Madame Lidoine undoubtedly esteemed her highly for in her journal she calls her her "right hand," her "daughter adviser," once even her "motherly daughter." And she mentions that after the death of the Prioress Croissy, she had hoped that Sister Marie de l'Incarnation would be chosen in her place. But that the Church had selected a "far lesser one." By this she meant herself!

"It is true that Madame Lidoine was quite insignificant both in appearance and in her religious life. This was especially evident in the period following her election. It was very difficult for her to acquire the habit of giving commands to those she considered above her, and so she gave the false impression of being uncertain." So said Sister Marie de l'Incarnation and she added: "This apparent wavering was a great temptation to me." (So she herself broached the sore spot of her relationship to the Prioress for there is no doubt that she dominated her.)

In this matter also the Reverend Mother did not actually contradict her. She merely handed her the letter of Monsignore.

Marie de l'Incarnation read it. Her expressive face

changed. She blushed and paled. One could see how greatly this communication of the restriction of membership in
the order affected her. When she had finished she said
with deep emotion: "What a difficult choice, Reverend
Mother!"

Madame Lidoine had evidently expected a different answer. She looked shy and timid as always when she had to
oppose Marie de l'Incarnation.

"Do you think it is a question of choice?" she asked in
her deep voice. (This voice was the most characteristic
thing about her.) Marie de l'Incarnation answered quickly
—she had the utmost sensitiveness and subtlety of perception: "You desire this investiture, Reverend Mother?"

"Monsignore wishes it," the Prioress answered almost
apologetically.

Marie de l'Incarnation submitted at once. (My dear
friend, it is touching to follow the efforts of this great soul
to attain complete humility.) "Under these conditions,"
she said, "I cannot, it is true, retract my opinion of our
postulant, but I shall beg God to accept me as a sacrifice
for her. Permit me, Reverend Mother, to assist the soul entrusted to our care by extraordinary acts of love and atonement, so that admission to our community may not en-
danger her in any way." (You know that in the Carmelite
convents such acts of heroic love can be accomplished by
one Sister for another, and undoubtedly Madame Lidoine
was happy to hear of Marie de l'Incarnation's pious decision.)

So the investiture of Blanche was decided upon. Now in
the Carmel de Compiègne they knew with absolute certainty that this event would be the last of its kind for a long
time to come, and so the ceremony was endowed with
poignant significance. But we must not fancy that the ma-

jority of the Carmelite nuns were at all concerned or troubled. The members of this order, which is often termed somber because of the severity of its penances, are usually as carefree and merry as children. At this time everyone in Compiègne was happy that, notwithstanding difficult conditions, they were to succeed in admitting another young Sister to the order of Carmel. The little novice Constance de Saint Denis expressed quite naïvely the idea that may have prompted the counsel of Monsignore: "Dear little Sister Blanche," she said, "let us hold together, you and I, and play a trick on the national assembly! We are young, and though it is sad to contemplate that we shall reach Heaven so late, let us hope to grow a hundred years old. For by that time new novices will surely be admitted to our order again."

In the meantime Blanche in her brown habit and the white veil of the novice looked just as frail and appealing as when she had first gone into seclusion. Surreptitiously, her hands trembling with happiness, she would caress the rough wool of her robe, and this gesture was so eloquent of her state of mind that the convent felt at peace about her.

On the evening of the day of her investiture, Madame Lidoine wrote: "The gratitude of our young daughter is indescribable. For the poor child knew very well that her strength was failing and had not been prepared to receive the veil. 'Oh, how good is His Majesty! How good is the Reverend Mother! How kind Sister Marie de l'Incarnation!' Again and again she repeated these words. When she heard the name she was to bear from that time on, she soon regained her composure. During the recreation in the garden she suddenly and impulsively fell on her knees in the olive grove where the Prioress Croissy had knelt so often, and lifting her voice in deep fervor, she publicly accepted her new name by uttering this prayer: 'O Lord Jesus, in this garden of Gethsemane I yield myself utterly to Thee!' "

"Because of her humble gratitude and because of the name which Heaven gave to this timid child, I am full of hope," so Madame Lidoine concluded. "O Jesus in the Garden of Gethsemane, this is my prayer also, strengthen the spirit of Thy young bride and send her a succoring angel such as attended Thee and gave Thee balm in Thy hour of mortal fear!"

And it actually seemed as if this time the hopes of the convent were to be fulfilled. They no longer suspected Blanche of simply repeating the heroic ritual of the Carmelite faith, nor did she seem to be oppressed by it. The young novice was as fervent as on the day of her reception and made such decided progress that even Sister Marie de l'Incarnation was satisfied. And because of this general confidence in Blanche her second relapse was all the more shocking.

But here I must give you a brief summary of events.

CHAPTER IV

I do not know whether at that time similar measures
were taken in other convents and whether they were connected with recent investitures, but the fact remains that
soon after Blanche had been received as a novice a commission arrived in Compiègne with the purpose of con-
ducting investigations as to the number, the age, and the
religious sincerity of the Sisters. For in those days the
authorities already intended to persuade the members of
religious orders to return to the world, that is to say, to an-
nul their vows, and they naïvely expected the majority to
throw themselves jubilantly into the arms of the triumphant Revolution.

Before the commission interviewed individual Sisters, it
made a survey of the entire convent. According to reports I
heard, I am under the impression that they suspected some
concealment or other. For since the publication of
Diderot's famous story, all our freethinkers were full of
fairy tales about imprisoned nuns!

They went from cell to cell and Sister Marie de l'Incarnation accompanied them, in obedience to the command
of the Reverend Mother. Probably these men did not walk
very noisily, perhaps they even walked with that uncertainty which the representatives of a new order usually feel
toward an old established culture. But they walked as men
do walk (and remember that these corridors were accustomed to the hushed feet of women!) It is likely, too, that
they did not wish to show any respect for their surround-

ings. (It is significant that the Choir Sisters had been
forced to raise their veils.) The faces of the men must have
expressed this lack of reverence but I do not believe that
they could have been especially threatening, for they still
hoped to bend the order to their wishes without the use of
violence. Marie de l'Incarnation told me that even the most
objectionable member of the commission, a bold little
fellow who obviously held an inferior position, was comi-
cal rather than terrible as he trotted along in advance of the
others, a red cap perched awry on his greasy hair, and
flung open the doors of the cells. I am sure he felt a shame-
less delight in penetrating the enclosure of a convent. But
as I have said, all this did not make him at all dreadful but
merely contemptible and bizarre. And yet he affected poor
Blanche with utter terror. For as soon as this absurd little
fellow opened the door of her cell and peeped through the
crack with a grin, she uttered a piercing scream. (Sister
Marie de l'Incarnation told me that in the worst days of the
subsequent revolution she never again heard such a cry.)
At the same time she retreated toward the wall of her cell
with outstretched hands as if she were warding off un-
speakable horror and when she could go no further she
stopped as if she were awaiting death.

The men stood still too, at first in surprise, and then
with growing interest. Apparently they believed they had
found the prisoner whose presence they had suspected. At
any rate the leader began to speak to Blanche with the utmost affability and tried to persuade her to give him her
confidence.

She was so terror-stricken that she could not reply. But
when, encouraged by her silence, he suggested that perhaps
she wished to leave the convent, a second terror broke the
spell of the first and she burst into a flood of tears.

The fellow was delighted at the prospect of saving a victim of religion and displayed great eagerness in a good cause. He told her that she might consider herself free, that the new laws permitted no more investitures. He was about to take her hand in a fatherly manner when Sister Marie de l'Incarnation intervened. Her beautiful eyes blazed at him in stern determination as she said: "Monsieur, you are exceeding your authority. As far as I know the law of which you speak has not yet become valid."

I do not know what his answer would have been if Blanche at that moment had not fled to the arms of her novice mistress and thus given him the clearest reply in the world. He saw that he had made a mistake and colored like a rejected suitor.

In the meantime the professed nuns stood grouped around their Prioress in the chapter room. Had she been taller one might have made the comparison of chickens clustered about the mother hen, but as it was, Madame Lidoine almost disappeared among her daughters.

One by one the Choir Sisters were called into the chapter room and to give more weight to the procedure, the entrances were guarded by soldiers. As she went, each Sister bade farewell to the Reverend Mother who counseled her to give brief but courteous answers, for such had been the advice of Monsignore Rigaud. Well, you can imagine that their replies indicated loyalty to the order. There were no difficulties of any kind. Only the interview with Marie de l'Incarnation was characterized by a short, stormy interlude.

It is my opinion that this would have occurred without the preceding episode in Blanche's cell. Imagine this tall distinguished woman of noble birth face to face with those proletarians! Picture to yourself a nun imbued with her mystic mission of atonement before those dry officials, and you will see that a clash was unavoidable, even if the way had not been paved for it. Of course, from a psychological point of view, the leader bore a grudge to this nun who had shamed him publicly. In his very first words he clearly revealed the desire to humiliate her by asking her contemptuously whether she and the la Force Sister had recovered from their attack of fear.

Marie de l'Incarnation knew that she had not been afraid but at this moment she felt a maternal and sisterly responsibility to protect the weakness of the poor little novice from outsiders. There is no doubt that she was seized with the desire to uphold the honor of the order which her young pupil had endangered and this explains the extraordinary boldness with which she faced the commission.

"What do you mean by the word fear, Monsieur?" she asked. "How can we fear anything but the thought of displeasing Christ, allegiance to whom you are giving us the honor to proclaim?"

This answer was, of course, calculated to increase the man's ill-suppressed anger. (It is always difficult for small souls to endure the profession of a faith alien to them.) Again he transgressed the limits of his power.

"You are mistaken, Citizeness," he replied. "We are not here to afford you the honor of listening to your fanatical profession but to ask you in the name of the nation whether or not you will leave this hotbed of superstition. But allow me to suggest to you that the representatives of the nation have authority so complete as to inspire a certain amount of that fear which you—wrongly, I believe—rejected just now!" Ah! the deluded man did not feel that this open hostility, instead of intimidating them, was kindling the fervor of these Carmelites. (For, my friend, Christianity thrives upon persecution and this is the reason why all brutality, crude or subtle, directed against it, becomes merely stupid.)

Marie de l'Incarnation divined the threat which a moment later she was to hail as a special honor conferred upon her.

"My profession of faith," she replied fearlessly, "contains my answer to your question. But as far as the authority of the representatives of the nation is concerned, it is only as great as God permits. Not an iota more! Let me tell you this, Monsieur!"

You can readily understand that these words added fuel to flame! "Very well," he replied, "I shall remember your answer. The movement afoot now is not yet at an end. I hope the day will come when churches and convents will be besieged as well as the Bastille. But do you happen to know what happened to the commander of the Bastille, Citizeness?" (He was referring to De Launys whose head, dripping with blood, the people bore on a pike through the city!)

For a second she was completely silent and motionless. Doubtless the man was already enjoying the satisfaction of having frightened her to death. Then slowly a flush of happiness mounted to her face.

"I know," she answered softly. "Oh, I know very well!" It was as if her voice were kneeling overcome by strange ecstasy. She crossed her arms on her breast.

My friend, we must stop to examine that attitude of the Carmelites with which we are both fairly unfamiliar. It depends so utterly on the concept of sacrifice of one to save the many, that in them the Christian belief in salvation by the Cross is transmuted into a fervent love of suffering and persecution. I know that it is hard for the non-Christian world, even for the world at large, to comprehend this idea, that it may even be considered pathological. In spite of this, I beg you to suppress your own sense of values and to accept the Carmelite point of view simply as a matter necessary for the understanding of this story. (Or rather for the understanding of all Christianity.)

"When I left the chapter room," Marie de l'Incarnation told me, "I felt as if a tall, solemn funeral taper had been lit within me, and its light suffused me so that I seemed to become entirely transparent."

And at sight of her the Reverend Mother said at once: "Why, you are aglow as an angel, my daughter. What has happened to you?"

She replied in a voice stifled by emotion. But her exultation broke through: "O Reverend Mother! Wish me joy! Wish us all joy! Felicitate this land and this throne! His Majesty will permit us to perform a penance we never dreamed of: they have threatened me with martyrdom!"

To her surprise Madame Lidoine did not seem to share her rapture. She only asked rather dryly how such an undesirable situation had come about.

Marie de l'Incarnation fell on her knees at once. She accused herself of having exceeded the commands of the Reverend Mother, of not having spoken with gentle brevity. "For," she told me, "at that time I had no lack of zeal to overcome my pride, but I had not fully recognized the seat of it." (The flaws in this great soul, my friend, lay so far beyond common shortcomings!)

And the Prioress replied at once, and I do not think that it was only because there were others in the room: "There was never any question of a command, my daughter, only of advice."

CHAPTER V

Meanwhile poor Blanche was still in a deplorable condition which I believe we may term a nervous breakdown. During this period, Sister Marie de l'Incarnation remained at the side of the young novice as her untiring nurse and companion. Now I fancy that the personality of this great nun must have been very suggestive and that the goal was reached the more easily since Blanche looked to her novice mistress with all the yearning admiration of the weak for the strong. And so, a few days later, she appeared again in the circle of the Sisters and was obviously concerned in atoning for the bad impression she had made in her interview with the commission. In the refectory, according to the custom of convents, she penitently accused herself of weakness and commended herself at the same time to the prayers of the Sisters. It was really astonishing that so much humility and good will did not prove to be more fruitful.

The outsider may say that it is not hard to understand that a young and somewhat delicate nun showed anxiety during the following period. For I remember quite well that at that time convents were robbed in various sections of the country. Such acts, indeed, were the natural response of the people to the decisions against the Church that had been made by the national assembly. Blanche had good reason to be concerned and she showed concern. She did not admit this voluntarily, but it could be recognized easily by little involuntary signs. When I consider the matter as a whole, I might even say that as far as Madame de Chalais' excellent education was concerned, a carefully wound-up ball of yarn was unwinding itself again. Or, to express it differently: the vanished little rabbit had returned and behaved exactly as it had years ago. As a child Blanche had asked continually whether the stairs would not slip from under her or whether people would not grow angry. And now, during the recreation, she would suddenly inquire in a small, agonized voice whether any new robberies had occurred or whether they would surely permit members of orders to remain in their convents.

"I am not at all afraid," she would say with a gallant gesture that was so pathetically false (and no one believed her little attempts at boasting any more), "no, I am really not afraid! What is there to be afraid of? If the King of France is powerful, how much more—" Here she was involuntarily repeating a phrase of Madame de Chalais' but suddenly she stopped, for she probably remembered how badly the King had fared recently when the people dragged him, a prisoner, from Versailles to Paris. The *Carmagnole* and the *Ça ira,* which sounded more and more often from the street into the convent garden, caused her discomfort too. She would suddenly ask the Prioress for permission to fetch a forgotten book—just as she had done as a child. She almost gave the impression that she wanted to hide somewhere, where she could not hear the singing.

"Dear little Sister Blanche, let's play a trick on the national assembly and grow to be a hundred years old," the young and naïve Constance Saint Denis said to her. "Let us survive all these horrid laws about convents. How can you spoil things for yourself by being so afraid?" And another time: "Are we not the brides of Christ?" And the old Sister Jeanne de l'Enfance de Jésus who was really almost a hundred years old, said: "Are we not servants of *le petit Roi de Gloire* and will He not give us strength and care for us under all conditions?" (The Carmelites did not say, as Madame de Chalais, *"Le petit Roi* will protect us," but they said, "He will give us strength"!)

At that time most of them lived in the same enthusiastic readiness as Marie de l'Incarnation, who now increased her prayers and her sacrifices for Blanche. (You recall, my friend, that she had pledged herself to do this before the too hurried reception of the young novice?) I have since hesitated to mention these sacrifices because I did not want to deprive them of their chief beauty—their complete secrecy. No one in Compiègne besides Madame Lidoine knew anything about them. Marie de l'Incarnation tried to conceal them from Blanche in particular. (In this curious nun we fathom new depths of religion again and again. She never tried to influence the novice entrusted to her care psychologically. She wished to work through sacrifice and prayer as she did in regard to the world itself, and to do this through God to whom she was offering her prayers. She knew only the ultimate in all things.)

In those days her influence in the community must have been extraordinary. I understood this: I really believe it would have been impossible for this woman to prevent her flaming urge to martyrdom from quickening others, even had she wished it. But she could not possibly wish it! Only remember the peculiar duty of her order, my friend! Do you recall how before the revolution the question would arise as to whether Christianity could still produce martyrs if the occasion presented itself? Later we learned the truth, namely that in this order martyrs were actually ready and waiting!

"France will not be saved by the zeal of its politicians

but by the prayers and sacrifices of devoted souls! Today is the great hour of the Carmelite Order!'' This was the chord to which the quiet Sisters of Compiègne were at-tuned in those days. They were deliberately preparing for martyrdom.

"Shall we really need these supplies?'' asked the naïve little Constance de Saint Denis, when the Reverend Mother casually inquired whether vegetables necessary for the winter had been picked in the garden.

"Why should we not need these things, my child?'' Madame Lidoine replied. Very often now she heard or rather overheard the question: "Shall we need this?'' Among her nuns it was an open secret that she was strangely aloof from the heroic preparations of her daughters.

"The convent is stringing bright-colored beads,'' she says jestingly in her journal, anent these preparations. And another time, "My daughters are again playing with the idea of martyrdom.''

Now, my friend, I am far from wishing to belittle the heroic frame of mind of these pious women. And yet I must mention the fact that at that time there was no pos-sible reason to believe in the probability of martyrdom. After all, the threats of an individual official were only a breach of manners in keeping with the impudence of the people. There were certain difficulties and limitations to be faced, perhaps a temporary dissolution of the order. But there was no dreadful issue at hand. Was it not a gross mis-interpretation to accuse these humane times of bloodthirst-iness? And was it not a little absurd to credit them with the awful crime of hating God, when in reality everyone was busy mouthing philosophical phrases and discussing press-ing questions of state finance? At that time we did not think of subsequent developments. So heroism was really an extravagant figment of the fancy and as out of place as fear—if you will pardon me my frankness. And yet we would err in ascribing these considerations in Madame Lidoine's resistance to the behavior of the nuns.

You know, my friend, that the command which Monsignore had anticipated came very quickly. It categorically prohibited the reception of new novices and also forbade those already received to make their eternal vows. (Try to imagine the grief of a young Sister at this ruling which condemned her to an everlasting novitiate!) In the Carmelite convent of Compiègne, in addition to Blanche, Sister Constance de Saint Denis was especially involved since she was shortly to take her vows.

At this juncture Marie de l'Incarnation emphatically recommended that she be permitted to do this in all secrecy, in the catacombs, as it were, just as Blanche had been received not so long ago.

"Is it so great a venture, Reverend Mother," she said to the Prioress with noble insistence, "is our daring so great, even if the matter is discovered? The sooner the world lets us feel its hatred, the better for that world!" (Do you observe here the slight change of attitude, the shift from mere readiness to the expressed wish? And you will, I believe, now understand Madame Lidoine's reluctance to share the enthusiasm of her daughters.)

At the time I was just speaking of, she surprised Marie de l'Incarnation by one of her first independent decisions. She rejected the suggestion with the somewhat depressing reason that on the occasion of Blanche's reception it had been the question of a prospective law, while now the ruling was in full force and she added that she did not think it advisable to rouse the anger of opponents needlessly.

This reason was of course not fundamental. I cannot resist describing to you how Madame Lidoine informed the two novices of the painful provisions of the new law. For here the veil of insignificance is raised from the soul of this woman who appeared so plain and usual to those about her. ("At that time," so Sister Marie de l'Incarnation told me, "she acted as a prioress for the first time and," she added softly, "in opposition to me!") Before she read the decree she prayed the famous hymn of her foundress Teresa of Avila, with her assembled daughters:

> *I am Thine, I was born for Thee,*
> *What is Thy will with me?*
> *Let me be rich or beggared,*
> *Exulting or repining,*
> *And comforted or lonely.*
> *O Life!—O Sunlight shining*
> *In stainless purity!*
> *Since I am Thine, Thine only,*
> *What is Thy will with me?*

Then she read the decree. "You, my daughters," she said to the two novices, "because of this cruel ruling will offer your vows to His Majesty by sacrificing the joy of pronouncing them openly. For it is not important," here the clear eyes of the Prioress fixed the Sisters, one after another, "to realize our own aims even though they may be most worthy, but to fulfill the wishes of God. Do not therefore rebel against this decree, my dear novices, but neither shall you try to suppress your sorrow by sheer force of will. Embrace your disappointment—and it is justifiable —in complete love of God, and you will be obeying the spirit of our order. You will be Carmelites in the full sense

of the word at the very time when the world does not permit you to be Carmelites!''

Well, my friend, this speech and the prayer which pre-
ceeded it, can be interpreted in many different ways. The
only question is whether it was understood.

If Blanche understood it—and Madame Lidoine observed that she listened with rapt attention—her understanding bore no fruit. Indeed it must be admitted that just
at this time her behavior began to be profoundly disturb-
ing.

CHAPTER VI

It was Advent and the old Sister Jeanne de l'Enfance de Jésus was sewing a new shirt for *le petit Roi de Gloire*. It was turning out a little awry, for her eyesight was almost a hundred years old. But she had not wanted to give up this beloved duty.

"Dear little Sister Blanche, now they will soon bring our little King to you," she said to the young novice, "don't you feel a little happy about this?" (You know, my friend, that *le petit Roi de Gloire* is carried into the cell of every Carmelite on Christmas night. Blanche, who had just been received, was to experience this ceremony for the first time.)

Unfortunately a decree of the national assembly arrived a few days before the holiday. It confiscated all church goods and robbed *le petit Roi* of His crown and His scepter. Clad only in his poor little shirt, Madame Lidoine bore Him from cell to cell on Christmas night.

"Now our little King is as poor again as He was in Bethlehem," the Sisters said happily. These good and gentle women were tireless in their efforts to transmute all anguish into joy.

Blanche was moved. One saw it clearly on her face. Tears were in her eyes and two great drops fell on the little wax figure that was laid in her arms.

"So small and so weak," she murmured.

"No, so small and so powerful," whispered Sister Marie de l'Incarnation, who was standing beside her. She was not certain if Blanche had heard her. She was bending down to kiss *le petit Roi* and suddenly she noticed that He had no crown! At the same instant the wild strains of the *Carmagnole* rose from the street. Blanche started violently—*le petit Roi* fell from her hands and His little unprotected head struck the stone floor of the cell—and was severed from the body. "Oh, *le petit Roi* is dead," she cried. "Now there is only the living Christ!"

In the course of the night she must have gone through a dangerous crisis for when the Feast of the Holy Innocents was celebrated a few days later—and on this day it was the tradition for the youngest novice in the convent to rule all the rest—Constance de Saint Denis, who was two years older, had to take her place. But the worst of it was that Blanche suddenly gave the impression that she was no longer struggling against her condition as before. Up to now her ardent efforts to gain greater courage and poise had been reassuring to her superiors. But now it was sadly true that her resistance was lessening if not failing entirely! Marie de l'Incarnation was convinced that in some way or other she was accepting the situation.

This it seems was the reason why, in the convent of Carmel de Compiègne, the advisability of urging the young novice to return to the world was duly weighed. For the novitiate is like a question which can be answered in the negative.

"My big daughter," so Madame Lidoine wrote at the time, "saw more clearly than I in this case. It will probably be necessary to retrace a false step as soon as possible. And," she adds, "poor Sister Marie de l'Incarnation! She had offered herself up entirely for this child. But His Majesty did not deign to accept the sacrifice."

She had Blanche summoned in order to tell her in person whatever she considered necessary.

Blanche came. Since the last crisis her face looked still

smaller to the Prioress, even a little older, aged! If one can
speak of age in the case of such extreme youth. And so her
features, or rather the pinched, tormented expression of
her features, seemed more apparent than usual. She must
have divined why she had been called: she was like a child
that is to be punished; and yet at the same time there was
about her a sense of being comforted, some final secret
certainty and willingness.

The Prioress was touched with compassion when she
saw her. "My child," she said gently, "I have a painful
communication to make to you. But first let us together
seek solace with God." She bade Blanche kneel with her.
Then she prayed the hymn of Saint Teresa and asked
Blanche to repeat it after her.

And now a strange thing happened. Blanche obeyed her
at once. With her small tortured voice that was almost
breathless, she repeated the words said to her until she
came to the place:

> *"Let me be rich or beggared,*
> *Exulting or repining,—"*

But at this point she continued:

> *"And give me fear or refuge—*
> *Since I am Thine, Thine only,*
> *What is Thy will with me?"*

She spoke very quickly, almost mechanically like one
who says words one has known for a long time. She obviously did not realize that she was changing the text of the
prayer. But the Prioress was keenly aware of it. At first she
was about to correct Blanche but the same odd compassion

she had felt before restrained her. Without touching upon Blanche's prayer she broached the subject at once.

"My child," she said, "I presume that you know why I had you called?"

Blanche was silent.

Madame Lidoine had not expected this silence. "I have always appreciated your humility," she continued, "and I am trusting this trait of yours to lighten this heavy hour for me, because this separation is no less painful for the mother than for the child." She embraced Blanche. But the silence was unbroken.

Madame Lidoine felt a slight embarrassment. "Do you think that I am doing you an injustice?" she asked a little uncertainly.

Blanche was silent.

Suddenly the Prioress said with unwonted haste: "I command you to speak, Sister Blanche! Am I or am I not doing you an injustice by sending you back into the world?"

Blanche knelt before her and covered her face with her hands. "You command me to speak, Reverend Mother," she said softly. "Well then, yes, you are doing me an injustice."

"Then your novice mistress is mistaken? You still hope to overcome your weakness?"

"No, Reverend Mother." There was something quite hopeless in her voice and at the same time a strange note of peace.

The Prioress felt as though suddenly all her standards were collapsing. "Look at me," she commanded. Blanche dropped her hands from her small tortured face that held only a single expression of endless depths. The Prioress hardly recognized her. A series of quite unconnected images suddenly floated before her: little dying birds, wounded soldiers on the battle field, criminals at the gallows. She seemed to see not Blanche's fear alone but all the fear in the world.

"My child," she said brokenly, "you cannot possibly harbor within yourself the fear of the whole universe—" She stopped.

There was a brief silence. Then Madame Lidoine said almost shyly: "You believe then that your fear—is religious?"

Blanche sighed deeply: "O Reverend Mother," she breathed, "consider the secret of my name!"

My friend, instead of discussing this most peculiar interview I shall quote the journal of Madame Lidoine. You have already seen that her notes which were for the most part purely factual could take the tone of religious revelation. Here they rise to the heights of mysticism. The very beginning of the paragraphs in question is clearly distinguished from all that went before. Instead of a date there is the heading: "The soul cries out to God." And the following is written in the form of a prayer:

"O God, who art wisdom endless and profound and that cannot be gauged! Illumine Thy servant in the office Thou has confided unto her. Thou knowest, O Lord, that I am ready to fulfill Thy commands instantly and as soon as Thou dost deign to communicate them to me. There is only danger that I may not fully understand them. Dear God, my reason I open to Thee like a book. Obliterate whatever is not pleasing to Thee and underline that which corresponds to Thy divine will. O Lord, can it be possible that Thou, who canst increase the virtures of man beyond the bounds of nature, hast also glorified a failing of the human soul in like wise? Is Thy mercy so great that Thou has divined and understood the weakness of a poor soul who cannot overcome it, and that this very weakness Thou has merged with Thy love?"

These lines refer to Blanche beyond a doubt. For soon afterwards she writes:

"Was it Thy will, O Jesus, to choose the timid temperament of this poor child, so that while others are preparing to exult in the dying of Thy death, Thou has communicated to her Thy mortal fear?

"Was this the adoration that was still lacking to Thee and was I about to deprive Thee of it?"

The next pages are concerned exclusively with this last question. But then we read:

"I have called upon Thee, O Lord, in complete submission of my will, my reason and all my strength, to make known to me Thy decision, so that I may clearly understand it. And so I do not believe that I can be mistaken. Thou art silent, dear god, and so Thou commandest me to keep silence also."

I think I am right in interpreting this last sentence as Madame Lidoine's decision to leave to God the question whether Blanche's fear was a part of her religious fervor. This reservation of judgment on her part would coincide with the practice of the Church in most cases of mysticism.

And so, for the time being, Blanche remained in Carmel of Compiègne. And under the direction of Madame Lidoine! For at this time she quite suddenly removed Sister Marie de l'Incarnation from the office of novice mistress and assumed its duties herself.

From this point on there is conflict between Marie de l'Incarnation and the Prioress.

It is of course out of question that there was any conscious protest. The soul of this nun could not possibly have
opposed her Prioress openly. She accepted her removal
from office with exemplary poise. Neither did her personal
humiliation alter her relations to the young novice. Sometimes she would say impulsively: "Oh, that timid little
thing! I think she would run away from a mouse!" But she
said these things without asperity and it is certain that she
never stopped praying for Blanche. One can only speak of
a conflict with Madame Lidoine if one recalls her view-
point concerning the prohibition of final vows. For the
time being it expressed itself only in a very justifiable concern about Blanche's sojourn in the convent. For now
danger was really in the offing. But just as before the attitude of the former novice mistress communicated itself to
the entire convent.

My friend, I do not intend to tabulate public events. You
have guessed that the period I am discussing was that of
the struggle for a lay code for the clergy, that is to say an
oath of allegiance of the clergy to the government. And in
the course of the Revolution this struggle degenerated into
persecution of the Church. So the attitude of the convent
of Compiègne to Blanche was quite understandable.

"We have no use for anybody now who will spoil our
happiness," said even the mild Sister Jeanne de l'Enfance
de Jésus. "Only think that next Christmas we may be cele-
brating in Heaven with *le petit Roi!*"

And the naïve little nun Constance de Saint Denis added
with precocious wisdom, "And if it should really come to
persecution, could we all say with a clear conscience that
we will be strong enough to bear it?"

"No, my child, we certainly could not say that," said
Madame Lidoine, who was just passing, in her deep voice,

"but fortunately it is not necessary. For if such persecutions should really occur, His Majesty will have to have mercy on those who are strong among us as well as those who are weak."

"But surely on the weak before all?" asked Constance de Saint Denis a little uncertainly when Madame Lidoine had gone. She expressed what they were all thinking and so no one answered but they looked at Blanche.

It is difficult to describe her as she was in those days. Madame Lidoine has left us no psychological revelations and whatever she had to say about the mystic nature of the case I have already quoted. Her notes contain only slight practical suggestions, such as this: "I have advised the poor child to continue seeking peace in fear itself, since God, as it seems, has no intention of freeing her from this emotion."

"Consolation in fear," "shelter in fear," "resignation in fear"—these are the recurring formulas of Madame Lidoine. She even advises Blanche to be "loyal to fear." I emphasize this last phrase, because, as far as I can see, it became decisive for Blanche. We learn that under the guidance of the Prioress she gave herself up to especial veneration of the Eucharist, "of the unprotected God," as Madame Lidoine said. She uttered this on the occasion of the first blasphemies that were suddenly springing up in Catholic France in mockery of processions and other rites of the Christian religion.

Even to the spectator it seemed a curious coincidence that the same spring that saw the coming of stormy conflicts between the Church and the State in France, was also witness to the beatification of the great French Carmelite, Madame Acarie. (You recall, my friend, that it was at her grave that Marie de l'Incarnation had first felt her call to the convent.) Naturally Catholics in France and especially the Carmelite orders of the country interpreted this event as the last solemn challenge to save the religion of the nation. In Compiègne too, preparations for the celebration of the new saint were made in this spirit. But let us discard here at once all illusions of pontifical masses or illuminations which usually accompany beatification. They considered themselves lucky in having a priest who had not as yet sworn the oath of allegiance to the government and who said a Mass honoring the saint. For the rest—they could not even purchase a worthy image of the new saint because all the Church money had been seized. However they found comfort in meditating upon the example the Carmelite nun had set her Sisters.

CHAPTER VII

It was May, and on the altar of the chapel stood the image of the Mother of God with *le petit Roi* in her arms. His little head had been restored but the great scar at the neck was painfully visible and there was, of course, no crown! Old Jeanne de l'Enfance de Jésus had substituted a wreath of flowers. You can easily imagine that Marie de l'Incarnation was particularly concerned with the celebration of this saint and felt dissatisfied with these modest preparations.

On the eve of the festival a messenger appeared at the turn of the convent and delivered a note which contained these words: "Reverend Sisters, tomorrow intercede with your new saint for him whose threatened crown defends that of your little King." The note was written by Madame Elizabeth of France and had reference to the King's resistance to the civil code for the clergy. (You know, my friend, how much this contributed to the fall of the monarchy!) It is unnecessary to say that in Carmel de Compiègne Sister Marie de l'Incarnation was most deeply stirred by this incident. Let us realize the essentials once more: she believed that she had been called to a religious life at the grave of Madame Acarie, to do penance for the sins of the court to which she owed her existence. The words of Madame Elizabeth must have affected her simultaneously as a challenge to her royal blood and her own most personal mission in life. At this instant she resolved not merely to prepare herself and the convent under her sway for martyrdom, but to consecrate herself to this martyrdom.

"The kingdom of France which ignored its true mission so often, has lifted the banner of Christ," she said to Madame Lidoine. "Permit us, Reverend Mother, in this struggle for the rights of the Church to offer it whatever help God allows us to give. Permit us to heighten immeasurably the celebration in honor of our new saint by offering the Majesty of God our own lives for the preservation of His threatened Church in France."

Well, my dear friend, I no longer need to assure you that such acts of consecration were entirely in keeping with the principles of a Carmelite convent, and, do not let us deceive ourselves, we must recognize in this state of mind the last and strongest reserves of Christianity in the face of ultimate peril. (For what does the persecution of Christians mean if not this: that the sacrificial death of Christ, which was a voluntary act, is repeated by the members of His mystical body. In this sense then no Christian martyr ever has death forced upon him from without!)

And yet at that time Madame Lidoine hesitated to give her consent. But she did not do so because she wanted to withhold herself and her daughters from sacrifice. Remember her attitude concerning the prohibition of the final vows. ("What is Thy will with me?") She only felt that this sacrifice had not yet been willed by God. And she justified her refusal by pointing to the possibility of some who were weak in the community.

Marie de l'Incarnation had understood. There was only one weak soul in the convent of Carmel! "O Reverend Mother," she cried with sudden passion, and at such moments the veins in her temples swelled as the rivers of France swell in a storm, "O Reverend Mother, why do you bow the heroism of your daughters under the yoke of weakness of this one poor child? Her name is la Force but truly she should rather be called *la Faiblesse!*"

"Her name is Jésus au Jardin de l'Agonie," Madame Lidoine answered simply. Ah! it was the tragedy of this woman that even in her most divine moments she remained so quiet with her big daughter, so devoid of pathos!

The pale ascetic face of Marie de l'Incarnation was stricken with sorrow: one could almost hear the rivers of France rushing in her temples. "I understand," she said with ineffable nobility, "Reverend Mother, you do not wish God to have at His will the heroism of your daughters but—" The word "will" had given her sudden pause!

"Oh, yes! Why not heroism too?" Madame Lidoine returned her question. But her words seemed intolerably slow and heavy to Marie de l'Incarnation. At this moment it was really most unfortunate that either consciously or not she had always overlooked the Prioress.

Well, dear friend, I do not wish to pry among the shortcomings of a great spirit. Low-growing trees are rarely struck by lightning; small white clouds breed no storms; shallow waters do not tend to destroy whole tracts of land! To speak in the language of my heroines: the devil gives important testimony, for verily he seldom seeks out small souls. Who can marvel that he prefers to be housed in lofty shining dwellings? Let us be honest: the Revolution was such a dwelling! My dear, both you and I hailed this new dawning of humanity and how cruelly we were disappointed! For the tragedy is not that chaotic impulses lead to chaotic conditions, that wrong thinking unleashes passions and crimes! The real and terrible tragedy of humanity is that at a certain moment her loftiest ideals (such as liberty and fraternity!) become a caricature and are transformed into the direct opposite of themselves. Of course this does not mean that all our ideals were false, but it does mean, my friend, that they were inadequate.

And now a frightful plunge! Before the outbreak of any

terror there is always a strange and solemn moment when
all who are concerned are suddenly aware of the inexorable
certainty of what is coming. Do you remember those
breathless August days before the downfall of the monarchy? (Ah, my friend, even a weak king is an incompar-
able bulwark of strength: not in the branches of a tree do
force and power reside, but in its roots!) Whence came the
sudden specter of Satan? This uncanny crawling approach
of the dark, the inarticulate? Who summoned it? Who told
us that it was inevitable? Who forced our humane con-
cepts, so confident of victory, to capitulate? Did it not
seem as if every leaf on the trees of France trembled with
us? All trembled! Those who craved horror and those who
resisted it desperately! But it is impossible to describe those
hours! One can understand them only if one has lived
through them, if one has shuddered through every frightful moment.

At that time Monsignore Rigaud informed the Prioress
Lidoine de Saint Augustin that he wished to speak to her.
Do not be amazed at this journey, my friend. The full rigor
of seclusion had abated in those days. Soon it was to be
abolished entirely. Members of orders realized clearly that
they were to be driven forth from their convents and monasteries. Even religious dress, that final, most intimate
symbol of seclusion from the world, had already been
abandoned. In response to the demand of the government,
the orders, devoid of all means of their own, had bidden
their members to apply to their families for lay clothing.

So Madame Lidoine hastened to Paris to receive the last
commands of her superior for the difficult times that were
at hand. She left Sister Marie de l'Incarnation to take her
place during her absence. You may be surprised at this ar-

rangement. I believe it was intended as a mark of confidence in her resisting Sister and also perhaps in the strength of her office.

And so the course of events seems all the more tragic.

We were just speaking of the inevitable certainty of all. But there was one person in Paris who was excluded from it. It was Madame de Chalais who came to Compiègne to bring Blanche the lay clothing she had requested of her father.

Madame de Chalais had changed very little. The solidness of her character and of her convictions had survived these troubled times as effectively as her too tight bodice triumphed over the new style of flexible waistline. It was infinitely consoling to hear how steadfastly she held to the idea that the exemplary piety of such a good king as France boasted of, could not possibly remain unrewarded. That if it really came to the utmost, the good Christian nobles and the Swiss who were gathered in the Tuileries would undoubtedly conquer the wild and heathen people and that Destiny simply would not allow the threatening of really worthy priests.

I assume that Madame de Chalais expresed herself something like this at Compiègne. Her interview with Blanche is not recorded but I do not think it was particularly important. It is enough to say that Madame de Chalais saw her pupil after a considerable lapse of time and, since lay clothing was worn, she saw her unveiled. I have already stated that it is somewhat difficult to describe Blanche but she must have had something very clearly defined about her, above all something utterly different from what Madame de Chalais had expected. I am almost tempted to believe that she enacted a scene with Blanche that was like the one that had taken place once upon a time at the banister of the stairs. At any rate, Madame de Chalais returned from the reception room in high excitement.

"Is it really true that you believe that one can no longer depend upon God?" she asked of the Sister who had charge of the turn. She was in a great perturbation. "Do you really believe that in a Carmelite convent? What a disgrace!" After these words she felt faint. They wished to call Blanche but she prevented them from doing this in great terror. So they gave her a chair and held smelling salts to her nose and gradually she recovered. But she burst into tears. No one could remember ever having seen her cry!

"O God," she sobbed, "O God, they will storm the Tuileries and drive away the King! They will depose him!" (Observe that she said "they will," and not "intend to"!) "They will kill him, the best and most God-fearing of all kings!" (Most God-fearing!) "They will slaughter the faithful priests" (faithful!), "they will murder the good Swiss" (good!). "Everything is wild chaos and we are making straight for the most terrible anarchy and the best, of course, will perish!" (Best!)

So she wailed to the poor nuns and in doing so mercilessly disclosed to them the desperate state of affairs in France. Obviously Madame Lidoine had kept the worst from them.

In order to quiet her they showed her a picture of *le petit Roi* but she hardly glanced at it. "Ah!" she cried, *"le petit Roi* is dead!" But she did not add as Blanche had done one Christmas night: "Now there is only the living Christ!" It seemed as if all her faith were suddenly at an end. Even her outward appearance was altered and dreadful. Her tight bodice was open. The whalebones had cracked when she sank into the proffered seat and jutted pitifully through the crushed silk of her dress. Her proud coiffure resembled a nest in which a cat has prowled. From time to time she fingered her gaunt neck as if to convince herself that it was still safe between her shoulders. Then she expressed her desire to travel to Switzerland, to Germany, Spain or Belgium. In short, in her imagination she fled across all the borders of her country only to return again to her own despair. But we cannot dwell further on the distress of this poor old woman. Suffice to say that they finally persuaded her to enter her carriage by telling her that if she really wanted to flee there was no time to be lost. (I heard later that she reached the border successfully but died in Brussels three days later.)

And now of Carmel de Compiègne! Imagine, my friend, on what ground Madame de Chalais' words fell! Remember that Sister Marie de l'Incarnation was taking the place of the Prioress! Without a doubt her office gave her the opportunity of initiating a step which Madame Lidoine had rejected, it is true, but not actually forbidden. (We shall never find Marie de l'Incarnation on the road of positive disobedience but always on narrow bypaths.) You have guessed which step I mean: it was a question of the last possible priceless moment for the heroic consecration to the salvation of France.

It appears that some of the Carmelite nuns were dismayed at Marie de l'Incarnation's proposal. For indeed it was no longer a matter of "stringing colored glass beads," to quote Madame Lidoine's words, for at that time the guillotine had already been established on the Grève Square. Nevertheless the convent consented bravely, though the Sisters grew more or less pale. Only little naïve Constance de Saint Denis confessed, half crying, that she would be very much afraid if she had to be the last to mount the scaffold.

This confession was very painful to Marie de l'Incarnation: "But you know that among the members of the order the youngest never goes last but the eldest, and besides you are not even the youngest but—" Not until this moment did she look at Blanche whom she had forgotten in her perturbation. "At this moment," Madame Lidoine writes later, "the shadow of Christ's mortal fear embarked on its voyage of heroism, but she did not recognize it!" This is an excuse for the erring of this noble soul but it is also a heavy accusation!

And yet Sister Marie de l'Incarnation felt something of that shadow. When she looked at Blanche she felt a strange oppression something like that of Madame de Chalais. But it was not the fear of sacrifice, it was rather the fear of hindrance to her own sacrifice. And now we reach the point when she knew: we cannot wait any longer, and also: we must be certain of our strength. For they were well aware that at some time or other they would be called upon to realize in action the words of the consecration.

"I am compelling no one to make this promise," she said quickly. "Whoever cannot overcome herself enough to offer Christ her life of her own free will, whoever does not feel this inexpressible ecstasy, let her remain aside." Undoubtedly she thought that Blanche would avail herself of this permission, and, let us be honest, she even wished it! For in this case, remaining aside meant excluding herself from the community, and so symbolized the first step to removal. But Blanche did not exclude herself and did not remain aside.

Let us briefly visualize the procedure of such acts of consecration. Personal vows are usually made silently during Mass immediately after transubstantiation. It is customary to inform the officiating priest. He refers to the vow of his memento and later gives communion and his blessing.

CHAPTER VIII

To continue again from the journal of Madame Lidoine. After her return from the city, this faithful and motherly woman did everything within her power to fathom the poor child's state of mind during and after the vow. The night before was spent in silent preparation. Now, my friend, we should greatly underestimate Marie de l'Incarnation's power over the human soul if we doubted that on the next morning all were in excellent condition. All, of course, except Blanche! Before going to Mass Marie de l'Incarnation made one more attempt to detain her. The emotions of the young novice can be inferred from her words on this occasion:

"My child," she said to her, "if you could only realize that no one is demanding this vow from you! Do you really wish to appear before the Saviour with this mortal fear in your heart?"

And Blanche replied: "Reverend Mother, I do not wish to be disloyal." (Let us remember, my friend, the formula that Madame Lidoine had underscored in her journal: "to remain loyal to fear.")

We know that Blanche entered the chapel with the others. Little Constance de Saint Denis who was walking beside her, recalls it distinctly. "But," she said, "I did not dare to look at her face, for on that morning we were all seized by a great oppressive happiness which made us very vulnerable."

And now the consecration itself! My dear friend, I still see before me a little chapel which the hand of the State had despoiled of all adornment, the altars empty as on Good Friday. I see a choir without chairs. In Carmelite convents there are no comforts. I see women kneeling on the wooden floors, women who are praying at a silent Mass accompanied from afar by the *Ça ira* in the streets. The faces of these women are strangely luminous. They are filled with the bliss of complete surrender, of unreserved and overwhelming willingness that has already passed beyond the pale of life and death. But I am like Constance de Saint Denis. Ah! my dear, there is one of these women I dare not visualize. I cannot endure the sight of a face small and pinched, wet with perspiration, distorted by terror—or rather by the terror of all France, of Eternal Love itself! Constance de Saint Denis relates that during the transubstantiation, that is to say, while they were making the vow, Blanche was still kneeling beside her. But when they rose to take communion she was missing! (Ah! hers was to be a very different communion!)

Well, my friend, none will gainsay us if we state that at the time Blanche's nerves failed her. But we could state the matter in quite another way too! "Poor child," writes Madame Lidoine de Saint Augustin, "it was she who wanted to share the mortal fear of the Saviour and when her strength broke, she ran into the very heart of fear itself!"

I pass over Blanche's flight, for unfortunately it is not only a question of leaving the chapel, but of quitting the convent. A few days later the Prioress received a letter from the Marquis de la Force in which he informed her that his daughter had reached Paris in a deplorable condition and was now ill. I cannot resist quoting at least a few sentences from the Marquis' letter. For Monsieur de la Force had suffered a change of heart no less astonishing in its way than that of Madame de Chalais! He had discovered that certain ideas were not content with furbishing his conversation with witty phrases, but had an odd tendency to demand realization with complete disregard as to the means to this end. As a result the Marquis was now all for a strong monarchy and absolute authority. He even surprised himself and his entourage by recognizing the need for religion and above all for the Church. The very first procession of the negators of God had shocked him profoundly. (Heavens! It is true that atheism is cruder stuff in the coarse hands of the mob than on the subtle lips of aristocrats!)

"This outrage is intolerable!" he is said to have declared at the time. "Something ought to be done about it! Religious people should see to it. I am told that they still exist in sufficient numbers. I hope they will increase. These circles are indispensable for the maintenance of law and order. Why don't they do something? Do the convents and monasteries believe that prayer and sacrifice will overcome these dangerous outbreaks? That would be a fatal error!" So Monsieur de la Force wrote to everyone including Madame Lidoine. But I am only mentioning this in elucidation of what followed. For unfortunately we can no longer ascertain whether the poor Marquis intended this time to face the results of his theories. For Life took the initiative and faced them in his stead, and as far as I can see, the actual events were the logical consequences of the beliefs that he had held up this point: early in September Monsieur de la Force together with many of his friends who were ardent advocates of freedom, found himself in prison!

CHAPTER IX

And now, my friend, I shall continue my story from a different angle, for from this point on I myself was a spectator of what I have to tell you. You know that in those days there was a rumor in our Paris circles to the effect that you too were among the imprisoned aristocrats. So, disguised as one of my servants, I hastened from one prison to another. I even wore the tricolor! But spare me a description of my state of mind! In the meantime your carriage was already approaching the safe shores of the Rhine. My friend, how I should like to refrain from reminding you of these things! But here it is not a question of conjuring up fear and terror or of satisfying perverse curiosity. Still, I cannot avoid doing these very things because it is my duty. My friend, fear is a great emotion. Not one of us was sufficiently afraid! Society should be afraid. A State should know fear. Governments should tremble. To tremble is to be strong. These things I am writing of have taken place and may reoccur at any moment!

It was pure coincidence that I happened to enter a prison courtyard at the very moment they were killing the Marquis de la Force. It was at night. The courtyard was filled with people. Did I say people, human beings? Never before had such creatures been seen in Paris! Where had they come from? What dreadful change had converted the populace into this bloodthirsty rabble? (Ah! my friend, this very change--that is just what we are concerned with!)

There was a pervasive reek of wine. Everyone was horribly drunk and filled with brutal and ghastly gaiety. Pikes leaned against the inner gates of the prison like a forest of stark trees. Torches burned at either side of the entrance and lit up this forest with a red, menacing glare. From time to time the gates opened and admitted one or more human forms. A sound of pikes, a few screams and all was over. (You know that this continued for several days and nights.)

I staggered from corpse to corpse to convince myself that you were not among the victims. The mob that followed the bloody spectacle desecrated some of these bodies most horribly. Again the gate of terror opened: the crowd was silent as a lowering animal. Suddenly I felt that no individual person was present at all. I could distinguish no one but the victims. Every time I tried to see one person alone, he merged with everyone else. Involuntarily I leaned against the wall to await the cry of agony of the only other person there besides myself. But I heard nothing. There was only a wild chaos of voices—then it stopped and there was breathless silence.

All at once I heard the short clear cry of a girl: *"Vive la nation!"* It was not loud but it penetrated to the marrow of one's bones. It was not a cry of fear but rather of love. I had never heard anything like it. Not terrible, but utterly strange, almost transcending. This cry sounded as if a soul had been released from matter and knew nothing more of the limitations of the flesh. I could not help opening my eyes.

The courtyard was filled with indescribable tumult. They were crowding about someone I could not see. *"Vive la nation! Vive la nation!"* the mob bellowed with fanatic joy. Then I saw how a very old man and a young girl were lifted on ready shoulders: they were Mademoiselle de Sombreuil and her father.

Well, my dear friend, you know the tale of this famous martyr to filial devotion, for the name of Sombreuil is included in your list of the heroines of the Revolution. Somebody called out out to me that this girl had just emptied a cup of the blood of dead aristocrats to the health of the nation! This was the price these inhuman scoundrels had demanded for the life of her father! In the meantime the gruesome procession approached. And it was a triumphal procession too! The two who had only just been threatened with death had become the heralded heroes of the people. They were carried by quite close to me. They say that Mademoiselle de Sombreuil had been a fair and blooming girl. I do not know if this was so. The person I saw seemed wholly bodiless to me. You will not believe me, but she looked ecstatic, as if she knew nothing of fear or disgust but only that her father had been saved.

The procession disappeared through the outer gate. The mob followed. An empty alley formed toward the prison: on the ground I saw the body of Monsieur de la Force and behind him, leaning against the wall, his daughter Blanche. A nasty little fellow in a red cap stood in front of her. Of course he was not the same one who had entered her cell, and yet through some infernal intuition he seemed to know who she was. Or did her rigidly folded hands betray the nun? Or her short hair? The fellow was holding a cup in his hand and made a blasphemous gesture. (My friend, you know of these things for you have seen the negators of God going about.) "Take communion, Citizeness," he screamed, and put the cup forcibly to her lips. Obviously it

was the one Mademoiselle de Sombreuil had just emptied
to save her father's life. Ah! my friend, she at least had the
significance of sacrifice to uphold her. Here there was only
meaningless brutality. Or was there a meaning after all?
Did this girl at that moment embody her martyred country
which was being forced to drink the blood of its children?
Horror of horrors! I closed my eyes again.

But already the mob shrieked its crazy *"Vive la nation!
Vive la nation."* It was over.

Some women near me grumbled, "But why don't they
lift up this fine young woman too! Is she supposed to walk
through the dirt?" (By "dirt" they meant the spilled blood
covering the ground!)

They lifted Blanche to their shoulders and carried her
past me in triumph. How shall I describe her to you? I
must confess that I did not recognize her at all! Her face
was completely devoid of expression, not bodiless spirit
like that of Mademoiselle de Sombreuil, but shrunk entirely into itself—gone! Her short hair that hung about her
face in frightful disorder seemed to me a symbol of the dissolution of her personality. (My friend, there is still
another death than the one Marie de l'Incarnation had in
mind.)

The crowd continued to bellow *"Vive la nation"*
without respite. A band of musicians joined in, the *Carmagnole* started up, everyone began to move. I felt that it
would be dangerous to remain in the empty courtyard and
joined the procession. A few women marched next to me.
They were the same who had called out before that it was a
shame to let Blanche walk through the dirt. They assured
me that they would accompany her to the residence of the
de la Force family and see to it that the little citizeness got

her supper all right. And I am sure that they really attempted to do this! Ah! my friend, do not think that these people were not capable of good impulses. The mob is always capable of good impulses! That is the very thing that makes a mob of people: that they are capable of anything at all!

As for me, I was convinced at the time that Blanche would not live through the night. This thought was a solace to me. But Blanche did continue to live—or rather to exist. If in that dreadful September night she had been the symbol of our unhappy country, there was in this continuance of suffering a sort of tragic rightness. How it was possible, I mean from Blanche's point of view, I did not know and in a deeper sense it is almost irrelevant. I might imagine that she herself knew nothing of her own existence any more. What actually happened to her is this: we have witnesses to the fact that she maintained her position of a favorite with the mob, that this most moody and changeable of all rulers continued to be proud of her deed. Ah! nothing bears greater testimony to the ruin of her personality than the terrible consideration accorded to her. If we are to believe a legend that circulated in Paris, the women were careful to minister to the needs of their young heroine. We know that some of them established themselves in the home of the murdered Marquis. They were seen there, their broad bodies squeezed between the gilded arms of the sofas, their knitting in their hands, the remnants of their meals strewn over the parquet floors. These meals they shared with Blanche. Then in the evening their husbands and lovers appeared. Such at least is my conjecture. The bloody events of the day were discussed. They sang the *Carmagnole*. They danced! Perhaps they even danced with Blanche. I seem to see her little hopeless figure going through the steps, as distinctly as I remember her on the shoulders of the mob on that September night. But let me say once more that fundamentally these details are not important, and that I cannot be positive about them either. Some say, and I consider this more probable, that in those days Blanche crouched in the corner of a rear room alone and in complete apathy; that only occasionally she was dragged out to participate in some mass procession of women or in some political parade through the streets of Paris. "We had to do that from time to time," I was told later by one of her dreadful September mothers who in the interval had become an honest market vendor again. "For the poor lady was an aristocrat by birth and besides she had been a nun and there were such fanatic people in the government. You probably remember, Monsieur."

Oh, yes, I remember! So it was merely a protective measure! My friend, nothing can exceed the loyalty of one of these September women!

And now this question occurs to us: Were these atrocities known in the Carmelite convent of Compiègne? I think it is fairly certain that this is not the case, but that the letter written by the Marquis de la Force was the last news they had of Blanche. (This is not surprising, my friend, for we are now launched upon the sea of chaos!) In Madame Lidoine's journal of this period there is no mention of the former novice. But neither is there any mention of the consecration of Marie de l'Incarnation and of Marie de l'Incarnation herself who had figured so largely before! This silence is most eloquent. It is broken only on the day on which the King was executed. Beyond a doubt the convent was deeply shocked at this event and interpreted it as a rejection of their will to sacrifice. Let us not forget that

Marie de l'Incarnation's dedication took place on the eve of the storming of the Tuileries—that for this woman of royal blood the salvation of religious France had always been bound up with the security of the crown! Madame Lidoine informs us that at that time she comforted her weeping Sisters with the words: *"Le roi est mort, vive le roi!"* By implication this referred to the unhappy little dauphin, for Madame Lidoine continues her journal with her own thoughts on this subject: "And so, O God, Thou hast permitted the king of our home on earth to become a small weak child like *le petit Roi de Gloire!"* And then with clear recognition of inevitable chaos: "It is then Thy divine will that we bring Thee a sacrifice without hope, unless that Thy ways be inscrutable!"

CHAPTER X

And now, my friend, we come to the preparation for the second act of consecration in the Carmelite convent in Compiègne. This time Madame Lidoine is the initiator. It is the preparation of inevitable sacrifice or, in her own words, "the sacrifice that is predestined"; but at the same time it is the preparation for unconditioned sacrifice. "Sacrifice without hope, sacrifice for God alone, sacrifice without heroism, sacrifice only through God, sacrifice in the dark of the night, a sacrifice in the midst of chaos"—these are the phrases that occur continually in her journal. She does not say "sacrifice to avert chaos"—this was no longer possible but what she had in mind is "sacrifice of absolute obedience" and "sacrifice of pure love." (My friend, I do not believe that she thought she was giving a new and increased value to sacrifice. This humble soul thought only of the special claims of her times.) Undoubtedly she was training the convent in this sense to expect a calamity. But what was the attitude of Marie de l'Incarnation to this altered meaning of sacrifice? I think it was already defined in the words, *"Vive le roi!"* Ah, my friend, in this slight remark the magnetic personality of that great Carmelite nun is revealed fully to us again! She was unbroken, unresigned! Obviously Blanche's flight to her father had relieved her immensely. I can almost hear her ask Madame Lidoine, "Reverend Mother, is it not a good thing that there is among us no longer anyone who might falter?" (The Prioress quotes this remark frequently. Apparently Marie de l'Incarnation repeated it often.) If we were trying to establish the presence of a sense of guilt in her, we might detect it in this oft-repeated phrase. But we can determine no guilt—at least no conscious guilt! This is probably the reason for Madame Lidoine's silence concerning the first act of consecration. She did not wish to anticipate an hour that had not yet been willed by God. But that hour had already come!

At this time the Carmelite nuns of the Rue d'Enfer found means to inquire of the convent of Compiègne if there was any possibility of sending *le petit Roi de Gloire*— or the sad remains of that little figure—secretly to Paris so that He might be closer to the little Prince, or "save him," as Marie de l'Incarnation said. (Ah! she did not realize what it signified that the dauphin was in the hands of the shoemaker Simon!) She herself had been called to Paris at that time by the authorities on the question of her income. (You recall, my friend, that this was her inheritance from the court.) Madame Lidoine writes that she hailed these dangerous summons with rejoicing because she thought she would have the opportunity of testifying to her love for Christ. Of course she consented at once, without any scruples or fears, to arrange for the transfer of *le petit Roi de Gloire* on this occasion.

The ancient Sister Jeanne de l'Enfance de Jésus wept at parting for she had been caring for *le petit Roi* for almost eighty years. On the very last day He was in the convent she had sewed Him a little coat for the journey (made of an old mended habit). Of course it was crooked again just as the shirt had been at Christmas. Still in the inventory of His wardrobe that was sent along with *le petit Roi,* it figured as "the mantle of the crown," just as in the past when it had been of purple cloth embroidered with gold.

Now, my dear friend, I must say that I consider it absurd to give credence to the rumor that this touching little inventory of His wardrobe which was later seized in the Rue de l'Enfer (*le petit Roi* Himself fell into the hands of His foes at that time) was the cause of the misfortune of Carmel de Compiègne. It is true that the accusation read: the nuns had attempted to hide the mantle of the crown and that the three poor little shirts all cut awry which accompanied *le petit Roi* had been destined for little Capet! But you know that such absurdities were daily occurrences. My friend, this mantle of the crown was only the cloak for an unpardonable undertaking. And in this accusation the name of Capet was used in lieu of that of *le petit Roi* Himself. The whole affair had already been decided upon when Marie de l'Incarnation was summoned to Paris.

The lawyer Sézille, who was her counsel during the proceedings, believed from the first that this business of her income was only a pretext to seize her person, since she was considered the most important member of her order; that this suit against her was simply the preface to other proceedings with which priests who had not sworn the oath of allegiance to the government and the members of dissolved orders were persecuted. (You know that the people had decided to reverence Reason alone! Ah! but Reason was betrayed as well as Faith!)

Lawyer Sézille feared for his client at the very outset. Perhaps he was also afraid of the passionate fervor she would reveal to the tribunal. At least I think this was the reason why he asked Madame Lidoine to come to Paris also. In spite of his misgivings, however, matters went off smoothly. Marie de l'Incarnation was too wise to give her enemies the triumph of appearing to have accused her with any semblance of right. She desired real martyrdom!

Monsieur Sézille admits that she faced her accusers with incredible dignity and consummate wisdom. And indeed she was quite calm. And this must have been the reason why the heart-rending news of the fate of the dauphin which she received in Paris, did not discourage her. (The Carmelites in the Rue de l'Enfer were only bent upon bringing *le petit Roi* to sick children so that He might help them to die!) It was certain that the Carmelites would be brought to court. Questions that were put, the manner in which the affair was drawn out and extended to other fields, revealed that there were ulterior motives involved.

Monsieur Sézille expressed this idea clearly, when, after the affair of Marie de l'Incarnation's income had been arranged, he accompanied the Carmelites to the stage coach.

They were in the Rue des Prêtres de Saint Paul, where it intersects with the Rue Saint Antoine. At this moment it was crowded with excited people. In the midst of the gathering the lawyer observed one of those carts in which the unfortunate victims of the guillotine were brought to the Place de la Revolution. In order to spare his clients the sorry sight, Monsieur Sézille cast about for an excuse to enter a nearby house, but the burning eyes of Marie de l'Incarnation had already seen! "No, Monsieur Sézille," she said quickly, "I see priests on that cart. Suffer us to gather strength by admiring the servants of Christ on their way to the place of execution! For you just implied yourself that we must hold ourselves in readiness to go that way also." Then turning to Madame Lidoine she added, "Is it not fortunate, Reverend Mother, that there is no one among us who is not ready to—" As she spoke, and it was the last time she defended her act of consecration, she suddenly grew pale and broke off in the middle of her sentence.

Madame Lidoine and the lawyer followed the direction of her gaze; it passed beyond the unhappy victims on the cart and fixed itself rigidly upon a group of women who had joined the procession. My friend, you know about those women who accompanied the carts to the guillotine, so I shall omit any comments.

"Christ in Heaven, now do I understand Thy moral fear," she cried, and immediately followed the procession and disappeared in the crowd. Madame Lidoine and the lawyer looked at each other in amazement. They waited a few minutes but Marie de l'Incarnation did not return. In the meantime the stage coach was ready to leave for Compiègne and Madame Lidoine had to make up her mind to go alone. Upon her return she was arrested together with the whole convent.

In the evening Marie de l'Incarnation reached the house of her lawyer in a condition of complete exhaustion. He was a dry and sober man—good heavens, he had to be for he was an excellent lawyer—but even he noticed at once that some great change or conflict had taken place within her. "She resembled a ship," he told me later, "whose masts move as in a storm although the air is quiet." Still she was able to tell him with outer calm that on that morning she had recognized a former novice of the convent among the women who were accompanying the cart, and that she had hastened after her to release her from her frightful companions. But her attempt had been in vain. The girl she was looking for had disappeared as if the earth had swallowed her up. I understand this: my friend, do you recall my feelings on that September night when I yielded to the gruesome illusion that there were no longer any individuals? Ah! chaos is a terrible parody on the equality of all! In chaos none preserves even his own face.

The small expressionless features of Blanche could no longer be distinguished from all the rest. It is remarkable that Marie de l'Incarnation had recognized them at all! Even if only for an instant! Now she herself assumed that she had been mistaken and seemed to find consolation in that thought. Nevertheless she asked her lawyer to make inquiries as to the whereabouts of the former novice, while she herself followed the Prioress back to the convent, a course of action which obedience, so she said, prescribed. But in the meantime it had become impossible to leave Paris. All the gates were under guard for several days, a regulation not uncommon in those times. Marie de l'Incarnation could not leave the city. And soon the news of the arrest of the Carmelite nuns of Compiègne arrived! Marie de l'Incarnation, who had been the very soul of sacrifice, was the only one who had escaped, who had been excluded from the sacrifice!

CHAPTER XI

At that time I had my first interview with her. Monsieur Sézille, who had come to me in the course of his searches for Blanche, took me to her. I did not suspect how much my memories of those September days must mean to her. She received me with the request to speak openly without trying to spare her. And this I did. My friend, I told her about Blanche's dreadful fate. She listened to me with marvelous composure but suddenly I saw that she had lost all control of herself. It seemed as if she were emptying the same cup of horror that had been put to Blanche's lips. When I related the incident to her she trembled from head to foot. It was a most peculiar experience to see this great and noble woman, whose every feature was marked with fearlessness, tremble so violently. I assure you, my friend, that never, not even on that September night, did I behold on the faces of the murdered victims so complete an expression of horror as on the most heroic lineaments I ever saw! It would have been insulting to offer her a word of consolation. I simply stated my conviction that Blanche could not possibly be alive.

She shook her head mournfully. (I felt that she had forgotten my presence entirely.) It was evident that at this moment she abandoned all hope.

"Oh, yes, she is alive," she said softly. "She is alive." And, with wonderful intuition, "Is not this poor country alive too? Is not the unhappy little King of France alive in all his agony?" And then as if she were plunging desper-

ately into the depths of her own despair: "It is harder to
live than to die! Life is more difficult than death!"

And now, my friend, comes the real sacrifice of this
great soul. We see Marie de l'Incarnation approaching it
and disappearing as through a dark gate—disappearing entirely. This sacrifice has no proud name. No one admired
her for it, noted it down or even observed it! (For the only
priest who knew of it in confessional will take his secret to
the grave with him.) Madame Lidoine's journal ends with
the day of her arrest, as may be expected. But Marie de
l'Incarnation's biography of the Sisters keeps utter silence
concerning herself. And yet hers is also a sacrifice of life
itself for she silently effaced the significance of her whole
life. And this significance was sacrifice itself!

Monsieur Sézille feared that she would try to rejoin the
Sisters. This would have been easy as there was a warrant
for her in whom the revolutionists hated both the soul of
the convent and her royal blood. (As far as men were concerned, martyrdom should have been meted out to her before all.) But we know as a fact that during the entire proceedings she did not take the slightest step that might have
endangered her, and submitted with admirable docility to
all the precautions imposed upon her by the lawyer at
whose house she was staying for the time being. He even
confesses that her caution was so painfully conscientious
that petty souls might have suspected that she was trembling for her life as the aristocrats were trembling for
theirs. She knew perfectly well what was being said about
her but she never made an attempt to justify herself.

The little singer Rose Ducor indeed, into whose house
she moved in the course of events (she suffered this pre-
cautionary measure too without resistance), insisted from
the very outset that this care on her part was exceptionally

saintly. (You recall that it was Rose Ducor who later spread the legend of the stigmata on the neck of her guest.) For Rose believed that the Abbé Kiener, an old Alsatian priest who also was hiding in her house, had impressed Marie de l'Incarnation with the duty of preserving her life. "Marie de l'Incarnation," so Rose Ducor said, "submitted to life as if it were a heavy penance." (Ah! Rose Ducor did not dream to what extent she was speaking the truth!)

To support her opinion she tells of that last greeting which Marie de l'Incarnation tried to send to Madame Lidoine. It was a narrow strip of paper on which were only these words: "Give me the crown of martyrdom or withhold it from me."

The resolute little singer who counted her admirers in all circles hoped to win over a prison official to transmit the message hidden in a ring. But she could not do it. (My friend, such plans only succeed in fiction. Real life is far more merciless.) And so in this direction also the sacrifice of Marie de l'Incarnation ends in profound silence.

In the meantime the Carmelites of Compiègne had been conducted to the Conciergerie in Paris. Their suit was approaching its end. I described the details in a former letter. The whole thing was just as brief as it was typical. In such cases the outcome was fixed in the beginning. I do not hesitate to designate such predetermined judgments as the darkest pages in the history of the Revolution. (But perhaps chaos cannot be termed history. It was something beyond all history.)

On the feast day of Our Lady of Mt. Carmel, these sixteen Carmelite nuns of Compiègne were condemned to death by the guillotine. Marie de l'Incarnation was included in this sentence. Try to imagine, my friend, what a storm of emotion this must have unleashed in her soul! Sézille informed her of the facts. He had done his honorable and hopeless duty in defending the sixteen Carmelite nuns.

Marie de l'Incarnation believed that her Sisters would mount the scaffold singing, for this had been prearranged in the convent. She begged the Abbé Kiener to be permitted to accompany him, for he had offered to give absolution to the condemned on the way to the place of execution. (Absolution disguised by the strains of the *Carmagnole* in the midst of the hooting crowd! That was the only possibility in those days!) But he refused her. "And this," Rose Ducor said later, "was a moment of most bitter sorrow to her."

"My father," she cried, bursting into tears, "you are robbing me of my last hope."

"And what is your hope?" he asked almost with severity.

At this question the full beautiful force of her personality broke through. She did not rebel. She was simply overwhelmed. "I wanted to sing too," she cried. "Oh, if I could only be the last, the very last for whom it is hardest of all!"

He answered, "Sacrifice your voice also, my daughter, yield up your voice to the very last one."

She wept again. "My father," she said, "my sacrifices have not been accepted. You know it. I shall be the most abandoned of all."

"Remember how Christ was abandoned," he answered gently, "and remember the silence of Mary."

Her resistance broke. "At that time," Rose Ducor reported later, "her face first showed that peculiar expression in which one could suddenly see how she must have looked as a child. It was as if an early, most lovely and delicate painting became visible under some splendid Baroque restoration." Without a word she crossed her arms on her breast.

And now, my friend, we have arrived at the question in your letter, the query concerning the touching voice of young Blanche de la Force.

Monsieur Sézille begged me to be present at the Place de la Révolution on that day. He wanted me to identify Blanche with the former novice, for he had learned that the women were going to bring her to the scaffold to witness the execution of the Carmelite nuns of Compiègne. (Another protective measure, most likely.) But do not think, my friend, that at this point I expect you to visualize the bloody guillotine! I myself cannot endure the sight of that horrible machine. Believe me, I had rather see a living executioner at work, a man who has the courage to wield the knife, and a hand of flesh and blood that knows at least that it is perpetrating an awful deed. Life should not be shattered by machinery. And yet this is the very symbol of our destiny. Ah! my friend, a machine cannot discriminate, it is not responsible, it shudders at nothing, it destroys indifferently everything that is brought to it, the noble and the pure as well as the most criminal. Truly, the machine is a worthy tool of chaos. Perhaps it is the very crown of chaos, a crown worn by the enthusiasm of the soulless mob that knows no divine creation but only satanic destruction.

I stood in the midst of the jeering crowd. Never have I felt the hopelessness of our position as desperately as then. You know that I am not tall. Chaos surged above me. I was lost in it. I actually could not see what happened. I could only hear. All my powers of perception entered in the sense of hearing and increased it incredibly.

The Carmelites arrived singing at the Place de la Révolution, just as Marie de l'Incarnation had expected. Their psalms could be heard from afar and penetrated the screams of the populace with strange clarity, or did the howls of the cruel audience cease at the sight of the victims? I could clearly distinguish the last words of the *Salve Regina* (this, you know, is sung at the deathbed of a nun) and soon afterwards the first line of the *Veni Creator*. There was something light and lovely in their singing, something tender and yet strong and calm. Never would I have thought that such a song could leave the lips of those condemned to death. I had been deeply disturbed. But when I heard this singing I grew quiet. *Creator spiritus, Creator spiritus,* I seemed to hear these two words again and again. They seemed to cast anchor within me.

And the song flowed on full and clear. To judge by the sound, the cart must have been moving very slowly. Probably the crowd blocked the way. I had the feeling that they were still far from the square. For this singing effaced all sense of time, it effaced *space* and the bloody Place de la Révolution. It effaced the guillotine and *Creator spiritus, Creator spiritus!* It effaced even chaos. All at once I had the sensation of being among human creatures again. And at the same moment someone seemed to whisper into my ear: "France is not only drinking the blood of its children, it is spilling blood for them too, its purest and noblest blood." I started. There was absolute silence on the Place de la Révolution. (My friend, even at the execution of the King there had not been such utter stillness.) The song seemed lower too. Probably the cart had gone on, perhaps it had already reached its goal. My heart began to beat.

And I became aware that a very high voice was lacking in the chorus—a moment later another. I had thought that the execution had not even begun and in reality it was almost over.

Now only two voices sustained the song. For a moment they floated like a shining rainbow over the Place de la Révolution. Then the one side was extinguished. Only the other continued to glow. But already the faded shimmer of the first was taken up by a second, a thin frail childish voice. I had the illusion that it was not coming from the heights of the scaffold but from the thick of the crowd, somewhere—just as if the crowd were making a response. (Lovely illusion!)

At the same moment the crowded lines were swayed by a violent upheaval. Right in front of me (just as on that September night) I saw an empty gap: I saw, and I saw exactly as on that night, Blanche de la Force in the seething mass of those dreadful women. Her small pinched face stood out from its surroundings and discarded those surroundings like a wrap or a shawl. I recognized the face in every feature and yet I did not recognize it. It was quite without fear! She was singing! With her small, weak, childish voice she sang without a tremor, exultingly as a bird! All alone across the great terrible square she sang the *Veni Creator* of her Sisters to the very end.

> *Deo patri sit gloria*
> *Et filio, qui a mortuis*
> *Surrexit ac Paraclito*
> *In saecularum saecula.*

Distinctly I heard the profession of faith to the Trinity. The amen I did not hear. (You know that those furious women fell upon Blanche at once.) And now, my friend, the rainbow over the Place de la Révolution had died away. And yet I had the feeling that the Revolution was over. (As a matter of fact the Reign of Terror collapsed ten days later.)

When I entered the singer's house in company with the Alsatian Abbé a little girl I did not know was sitting on the steps. She came up to us confidingly and produced a small bundle she was carrying under her apron. She handed it to the priest: it was *le petit Roi de Gloire!* The child had found Him in the street covered with mud. Someone in some blasphemous procession must have thrown the little figure away.

Together we went to Marie de l'Incarnation. She looked like a Mater Dolorosa. The priest took her hand. "Come, Marie of the Incarnation," he said. In his native language the significance of her name became more evident. Or was he speaking with special emphasis? He drew her over to the cabinet where Rose Ducor had concealed a little shrine of the Madonna, opened it and laid down *le petit Roi de Gloire.* Then he began to pray. He prayed the *Regina coeli laetare,* the Easter greeting to the Mother of God.

I prayed too. In that hour I was like a child who drops through all the layers of being to the very foundation of all things which is a foundation everlasting because it belongs to God.—And now, my friend, it is your turn to speak!

In your warm eyes I seem to see two tears. They are falling on your grave hands. Your lips are closed, I might almost say, folded. You are moved but you are disquieted and I know why! You expected the victory of a heroine and you saw a miracle in one so weak!

But is it not this that kindles exeeding hope? The human element is not enough, not even when it is "admirably human," as we said so enthusiastically before the Revolution. (Ah! my friend, fundamentally this whole epoch teaches us only what we have already learned from poor little Blanche.) No, the purely human is not enough. It is not even enough to offer as a sacrifice. My friend, up to now the bond that existed between us included a union of ideas. Can you endure the change in your friend? Well—it is your turn!